The Whistler

Marilyn Gwizdak Greenwood

For Lilian Violet, Daphne Athenais & Henrietta Galene

The name "Gwizdak" originated from the whistle used to command the Tartar cavalry. Our forefather, the first to bear this name, arrived in Poland as "The Whistler" in Genghis Khan's Mongolian army.

"The Whistler" is a wind that sweeps down from the Russian Steppes and blows across the flat plains of Northeast Poland.

Whistling is also a familial habit.

"*I have been forced to eat bread from many bakeries.*"

Jozef Jan Gwizdak (1923-2010)

This book is based on the memoirs of my late father Jozef Jan Gwizdak and is a true story of terrible human plight and endurance. This is Poland's unknown holocaust – the lesser-known history of a nation. It tells of atrocities faced by ordinary people, a fight for survival through great adversity, but also the loss of so much more.

And now the world should know…

CONTENTS

PROLOGUE. DECEMBER 1939

I am Andrzej Gwizdak. I am 42 years old. I am soaked to the skin, freezing cold and so tired that I cannot think straight but my worries concern me more. Where are my wife and children? Are they safe? I can only hope and pray that they have been spared.

I have been a prisoner in this monastery for the last three months. Accessed only by a long bridge, it is situated on an island in what is said to be one of the purest lakes in all of Eastern Europe. We are told that the monastery itself, with its many domes and spires, lays claim to being one of the finest examples of Neo-classical architecture in the entire region. Nevertheless, why should any of this matter to me? I am a military man, a family man, a landowner and a farmer, not a landscape artist.

The thousands upon thousands of hectares that make up this vast alien wilderness are nothing to me in comparison to a handful of my own soil from my native Poland.

I suppose that in another world, or at another time, this area would be regarded as a place of beauty; not during this particular winter though. At this moment, beauty is difficult to contemplate. Deep feelings of defeat, and above all raw fear, generate only ugliness.

There is an air of uncertainty permeating everything here

and I sense suspicion and a level of nervousness I have not experienced in a long time. Our days and nights are taken up with an unrelenting cycle of hard labour, exhaustion and repeated interrogations.

I am only too aware that the only words I will ever speak in the presence of my captors are not ones they want to hear – and I can never sway. It is not stubbornness; it is a primordial sense of who and what I am. Most of my fellow comrades are, likewise, amongst the most loyal and staunchest patriots that Poland will ever know, and we are of the same iron temperament. We are united in our mental battle, a battle that I struggle now to believe will ever end in victory.

We are left with only a dread of the unknown. Old soldiers die hard, but we are beginning to be worn down. In the damp darkness of our prison, when sleep evades even a spent body and mind, the Baba Yaga of childhood returns to haunt the mind of even the toughest of us.

Europe is at war again. I have been involved in three wars now in just over twenty years, and for me "enough" has lost all meaning. As I sit and contemplate the last twenty-one years of my life, a life that has now been violated and swept away, I remind myself that my memories can never be sullied. They can never be taken away.

As I wrap this coarse wool blanket tighter around me and prepare to lie down on a cold slab, my breath exhales in white clouds as my mind travels back in time, to a time exactly half a lifetime ago.

Before all this.

Before the world turned on itself, yet again, and started devouring its own tail

1. POLAND 1918

The Great War is over

Andrzej Gwizdak eased the rifle off his shoulder and propped it against a wall. He had carried it for what seemed like forever but he could not imagine letting it go even though he no longer needed it. Only two things had been so vital to him that he slept with them by his side: his gun and his tobacco. But now the war was finally over.

He opened his kit bag, took out a tin and began to roll a cigarette. He sat down on the bag to think. No more battles and no more killing. Could anyone outside of it imagine how desperate and unearthly this war had been? His experiences had chased away any remnants of boyhood and left his mind in turmoil.

These days, nightmarish mental images caught him unaware; they disappeared in a flash but left him unsettled. He was becoming accustomed to these subliminal, fleeting shadows and the morbid feelings they left behind and he knew that he needed a period of normality to recover. It was time to come to terms with everything and to heal.

As he looked down, he reflected that his boots had not been free from bloodstained mud for a long time. He remembered all too vividly the areas of heavy fighting. He had brought the evidence with him.

A man could trudge for miles on these great expanses of brackish quagmire where body parts jutted from the earth, limbs lying broken like discarded farm machinery, rivulets of red water trickling through fissures in deep mud, a nightmarish landscape of blood and bone.

During the long winter months, hordes of fighting men would run with heads down, not just to dodge bullets but to look out for the foaming, dark ice that was not frozen water but frozen blood. This stuff was thin and fragile because of its high concentration of salt. It could break easily under his weight and send him down into a deeper pit and God only knows what else.

Andrzej could not remember a day without the acrid scent of burning wood. Would the smell of scorched pine be forever trapped in his nostrils? He was, even now, gagging on that musty, choking odour although there was no smoke to be seen. He had to clear his head of it all and start to move on.

Hundreds of men were now spread out in an area of open countryside with little shelter. On the ridge of a nearby hill, silhouetted against heavy storm clouds, a long trail of dishevelled soldiers, a dreary cortege, trudged in line. All of them spent and weary, dragging their feet in an unpurposeful gait, unsure where they were going or what to expect.

Their elation had evaporated all too quickly, leaving many of them insecure and uncertain. The war had taken many a boy soldier and turned him into a man, but his passage had been earned in the most brutal way possible. How did a person move forward after years of living in this hell on earth? They would have to bide their time and await the return of calm and hope; hope for a future and a new start. Day by day they would re-form and gather together, feeling numb and almost unable to believe that the war had finally ended.

It was a grey day with little visibility and it started to drizzle. Andrzej pulled his cap lower over his eyes and turned up his collar. He spoke out boldly to anyone in earshot, "Well, I am twenty-one years old and my life starts now." He ground the roll-up under his heel, wondering why he had lit it in the first place. Looking up, he saw two of his compatriots, Leon and Stashu, coming towards him along a farm track. He nodded to them.

"Andrzej, get up." Leon came towards him. "Now!"

"What?"

"Real chicken soup. Down the road."

"Shift yourself," said Stashu. "Before everyone and his dog finds out."

"Let's hope no feathers this time, eh?" Andrzej started whistling as he collected his things and the three friends made their way down the track.

They had to hop to one side to make way for a horse and cart carrying wounded men. Andrzej fell silent. A man wailed pitifully. A soldier with a bloodstained bandage over his eyes leaned over the side and vomited, splashing their boots.

The men continued on their way.

"Well, we've finally got our country back, lads," said Leon.

"So what do you think it'll mean for the likes of us?" asked Stashu.

"What, Poland back on the map after more than a hundred years? Yep, does make you wonder what changes there'll be," said Andrzej.

"Have you ever considered how we can be Polish without a Poland?" asked Leon.

"A nationality but no nation?" said Stashu. "Never thought about it much. I just know I'm a Pole, that's all."

"No Poland for over a hundred years?" said Leon. "Has it been that long?"

"Tak!" said Andrzej positively.

Leon kicked away a large pinecone lying in the road. For a big, slow man, his footwork was deft. "So what do you think makes us Polish?"

"Dunno, can't think, I'm starving," said Stashu.

Leon laughed. "You can tell Stashu's a Pole. Like me, he eats for Poland." Stashu gave Leon a friendly thump on his back.

Andrzej had been dwelling on this only recently and reckoned he had his answer. A Pole is a Pole and proud to be so, and none more than Andrzej. The First World War had made him strong and resilient and now more than ready to carve a life for himself out of anything that might be thrown his way.

As the three young soldiers turned the bend in the road, they saw a swirl of smoke rising and spotted a young woman. She was standing over a roaring bonfire holding wooden tongs like those their mothers had used back home when doing the washing.

They stood and watched as she grasped bits of torn uniform and bloodied dressings from a heap at her feet and threw them onto the fire. The damp material hitting the heat and the effects of the drizzle, belched clouds of Brownian motion from the fire.

The young woman looked tired, but this did not mask her youth and prettiness. Tendrils of dark hair were escaping from her chequered headscarf but there was not a blemish on her long white apron. As she lifted her arm to mop her brow she saw them and extended the gesture into a friendly wave.

"What a looker," said Leon. "Get a load of that."

"Wouldn't mind her nursing me." Stashu crudely gestured with his hands.

Andrzej rolled his eyes. "Is this the way to the cookhouse?" he asked, though he knew full well it was.

"Tak." She stopped and pointed down the road. "Turn left at the gate."

Then Leon spoke, "Dziekuje. What's your name?" She looked at Leon and gave him a dazzling smile.

"Anka," she replied.

Leon turned to his mates and said, furtively, "Eyes off, she's mine."

"Nice to meet you, Anka."

"Thanks, Anka."

"Bye Anka."

The three young men took their leave. Anka smiled and shook her head at their comical display of excessive politeness. These young soldiers, they were all the same.

Andrzej was reminded of his own provenance as they passed a large wooden barn and outhouses now in use as a makeshift field hospital. The smell emanating from the area reminded him of an abattoir. His memory flew back to his childhood, which was vividly evoked by the odd power of a familiar scent.

He remembered when he and a friend had climbed a wall to peer over the top and watch a cow being cut up. There was a flash of steel and something resembling warm porridge poured out, steaming; and yes, that smell.

"That place stinks," Stashu nodded towards the barn.

"We're lucky," said Andrzej.

Recent experiences had not lessened their pity and revulsion at seeing men in the field carved up like butchered animals. They realised that they had not toughened up as much as they thought.

Leon broke the brooding silence. "Those poor devils in there won't be going anywhere in a hurry. Some heroes, eh? Destined to a life of no money and no women. A bit of metal on a ribbon doesn't compensate for losing your legs, does it?"

They arrived at the mess hall and, as predicted, just managed to get their soup and a bench before the masses converged.

Stashu eyed up everyone's portion before they even started to eat. "Do you want all that bread?"

"Yes, I bloody well do," said Andrzej as he broke all his bread and put it in his soup in mock haste. "There, all mine."

"Spit in it quick before he nicks it," said Leon, who laughed the loudest at his own joke.

Stashu slurped his soup loudly.

"You eat like a pig," said Leon.

"Well, at least I don't look like the arse-end of one."

The men grinned at each other, relaxed in the camaraderie that allowed them extreme insults without the slightest offence.

Silence reigned only for a few minutes more, as the men finished their meal. Their earlier conversation then resumed.

"So, do you think we'll all have to prove that we're Polish?" Stashu said as he stood up, eyed the queue and assessed the possibility of second helpings.

"What, because of land rights and things like that?" asked Leon.

"Well, there'll be a new government and a lot of re-organisation, so who knows?" said Andrzej.

"How many generations do you have to go back before you can say what you are?" asked Leon.

"No idea," said Stashu, only half-listening.

"So what makes a Pole?" asked Leon. "My mother was born in Russia."

Andrzej produced a piece of paper from his pocket. "I have a printed thing here. I think it's interesting."

"Who's it by?" said Leon.

"One of those war-writer, poet types," said Andrzej.

A smiling, chubby, young girl handed Stashu another soup. "Here you are, soldier-boy."

"Thank you my darling," said Stashu, almost theatrically.

"How's he got that? Bloody cheek," said Leon. "Anyhow, did you hear that, Stash?" He nodded towards Andrzej. "He's reading poetry now."

Andrzej ignored them and continued. "No, listen to this:

What is a Pole? A Pole is not just a person of Eastern Slavic descent but also a member of a unique race possessing a passionate determination. Poles distinguish themselves with an unusual culture, born out of a struggle to belong, to be a native in the land of their ancestors..."

"That's enough." Leon got up. "Andrzej will be standing for the Sejm next."

"I didn't get what half of that meant." Stashu got out his tobacco. "Let's go and see if we can find something to drink. I fancy some vodka with my smokes."

Of the three men, it was obvious that Andrzej was the thinker. He identified closely with the young Pole who had written these words while sitting up to his shins in mud and blood on the front line. It continued:

A Pole is not only a person whose first language is Polish, but who has had rhymes as old as time crooned over his rope-strung wooden cradle. Who falls asleep still hearing the music; traditional songs played on an accordion, whose sound can be as big and exciting as an orchestra to a small child.

A complex people who relate tenacious stories carrying such colour, they are almost tactile. A race that toils hard in the never-ending quest where more is never enough.

A language, often spoken in baritonal lilts and sometimes sounding over-assertive to an outside world, due to strings of hard consonants starved of vowels.

A people who, at times, can be too analytical of everyday things, resulting in giving extraneous dimensions to the simple and the ordinary. A Pole is all these things and more.

Andrzej quietly put the article back in his pocket, knowing that this was much of who he was.

"Anyway, where's this vodka coming from? I'm skint," said Stash. "You could get a few zlotys for that watch, Leon."

"Sorry, no go. Last thing I own. Not worth much anyway. Only thing my father left," said Leon. This reminded the three of them of Poland's hard times before the start of the recent war. Now they would hope for better times.

The canteen was overflowing, full of the raucous laughter of men, of steam rising from food and the foisty smell of unwashed bodies and long-worn uniforms. A soldier in the far corner of the hall started to sing an old, traditional Polish song and in no time his entire table joined in. This never failed to strike a chord in every soldier. The room filled with voices.

"Funny how most Poles are good singers, aren't they?" said Andrzej, his voice rising above the noise.

"We sing with the same passion that we defend our country," was the response of an older soldier edging past their table.

Andrzej and Leon wouldn't have minded hanging on a bit but they knew that Stashu was the one in a million Pole who couldn't sing and had often been compared to a constipated bull. Unfortunately, this did not deter him when he was in the mood so the men picked up their belongings and took their leave. Andrzej and Leon stopped by a table of men they knew, just catching enough of a joke to appreciate its punch line. There was a roar of laughter. Meanwhile, Stashu had crossed over to the serving area where he was whispering in the ear of the chubby, young woman who had finished serving the soup. He left her blushing and giggling, with a coy look on her face.

Stashu caught up with them at the door, "That's it. We just need to get Andrzej fixed up now."

Their boots crunched on the gravel path outside. They turned into the lane and the backs of three uniforms disappeared into the heavy, wet mist.

2. POLAND 1920

Another war

The Bolshevik Army had already started to mass on the eastern borders of Poland. The threat of another war was looming. Andrzej, along with his compatriots, picked up his firearm once again to defend an only recently repossessed Poland.

"How long this time?" Leon Badowski, having only of late shared his hopes of starting his own smallholding, looked desperately disheartened. "What happened to peace, Andrzej?"

"We'll just have to put our plans on hold for now, Leon." Andrzej was trying to placate his friend. "God knows, we are all sick of fighting." He instantly knew his words had fallen short. Leon was a few years older and desperate to put down roots.

Sadly though, a life of their own would now have to wait once more; Jozef Pilsudski, their leader and mentor, needed their support to defend the only thing that would ensure them of any future at all.

The Polish/Russian Front in North East Poland

Mortar fire had rained down upon them for more than

ten hours now. The return fire had been just as ferocious, if not worse, but the psychology of warfare does not allow the mind of a soldier to consider the folly of his aggressor. The men were hungry, soaked to the skin and cold.

"Badowski! Alert Sergeant Gwizdak and his fire-team, we need back-up here immediately."

As soon as Staff Sergeant Reydych had finished barking his orders, he heard, "Sir, I don't know how much longer we can hold on."

He glanced around, looking for the soldier who had just called out. He spotted him as he fell, the top of his skull blown open. The man was unrecognisable, with blood and dirt covering his face.

"Watch out!"

An almighty explosion followed and men were thrown high into the air, backs arched and blood spraying. To those watching, they seemed to be held in mid-air for the briefest of moments before their broken bodies slumped into the mortar hole that was to be their grave.

A gust of wind cleared the fog of cordite. The coppery smell of spilled blood filled the air.

All around was mayhem and slaughter and the fight seemed impossible. But there was also a powerful undercurrent of rage that the enemy state could again deny them a home, a land, somewhere to exist. They would fight to their deaths.

"What else is there?" "What have we got to lose?" These were words heard everywhere.

"Sir, I think we've had it!"

Their leader barked, "Then don't think, just fight. There's no room for thoughts of defeat. That's a word we don't acknowledge. Men, stay with me, keep the faith and by God we'll win this day!"

Sgt Andrzej Gwizdak and his men had left their defiladed position and were crossing exposed ground. Foxholes and the smoking, blackened remains of spruce trees hindered their progress, as did the wounded and dying men, many of them crying out.

As their boots sunk into the sodden earth, clods of mud splashed in their faces as mortar shells hit the ground nearby. The wooden walkways over mud too deep to pass were bombed and broken. The men fell and struggled to stand as they tried to protect their weapons by holding them above their heads.

The pandemonium was unrelenting. Ears rang and buzzed from the perpetual blasts. Even in their temporary deafness, the "whish, whish" of near-miss bullets could be felt, keeping the adrenalin pumping and the raw fear alive, giving the men that sickening but much needed edge. Another of their men went down.

Andrzej called, "Michalski, grab that ammo." Michalski briefly disappeared through a wall of smoke and reappeared, beating out flames on a blood-soaked canvas bag.

"Got it, Sarge." The loss of a man had to be absorbed but the equipment was irreplaceable.

Every man knew that he must brace himself to ignore the desperate pleas for help and outstretched arms of fallen men.

Against all odds, as they flinched and ducked at the scream of every shell, they made it to the other side of the hill. As Andrzej approached his men he stopped short, transfixed, gazing at the ground. His men wondered what the hell he was doing. Only a fool would stand still in this mayhem. Andrzej did not move. He was staring at a watch, still clasped to a wrist. Like a man crazed, he began to pull at the arm protruding from the mud. The arm came away in his hand and he staggered back, clutching it. An old soldier grabbed Andrzej and pulled him down, out of the way of another shell.

Andrzej had known instantly. Not only had he recognized Leon's watch but he could also see that the top of a little finger was missing, the outcome of an accident Leon had had as a small boy.

The men regrouped and took up their positions with renewed vigour.

The shock had hit Andrzej like a bayonet strike. His heart raced and in his panic he could not control his breathing. His mind was in turmoil. Oh no. Oh God, no. Instantly he checked himself; he must calm down and control himself or he would run the risk of joining his friend.

Later that evening, the men were able to pull back and have something to eat. The group sat around a large fire, exhausted, bone-cold and shivering.

A voice was heard calling out from the shadows "Do you realise that fire is saying "Here we are, come and get us?"

One of the men called back: "Get shot or die of cold, which is quickest?"

There was a need to talk about their losses and the conversation turned to Leon Badowski.

Andrzej joined the group. He was in a dark place. He could not shake off his profound sadness. They had been through too much, the recent almighty war and the experiences they had shared, some too terrible to recall. Then Leon's round, laughing face leapt into his mind's eye and the thought of this great friend warmed him and made him smile but only increased his grief.

"He was like a brother to me. I remember when I first got to know him. I was only a young kid. I hadn't been in the army long and I'd lost all my rations in the field. I'd just met Leon a couple of days before." Andrzej paused as the words stuck in his throat. He took a deep breath and continued. "Anyway, I'll never forget, as soon as he knew he split his supplies and shared them with me until we were able to get our next issue."

"Yeah, and everybody knows how much Badowski liked his food," came the response, as the rest of the group nodded and acknowledged the memory of the big man with a thoughtful nature, who was always hungry.

Andrzej had got to know him better over the years they had fought together. He remembered Leon saying once that he had a rough time as a child and that there was never enough to eat. He had once related to Andrzej that he could not forget the pain of trying to sleep on an empty stomach.

"He was a really decent bloke." Andrzej smiled and reflected that Leon had also shared his tobacco. Now that was a real mate. He also remembered how Leon had felt when he did not get promotion in the army, as Andrzej did. This was because his education was limited and he was only semi-literate. This had made the big man feel small.

Misery descended on him and he fought hard to shake it off. They had argued recently over some silly thing. He could no longer remember what it had been about or why he had thought it important.

Andrzej found a quiet place and stretched out with his arms supporting his head, his eyes fixed on the night sky. Although their companies had been split and Stashu had been posted miles away, he wondered if he would sense what had happened. He instantly told himself that this was stupid.

He thought back to the time in the Great War when they had met: Leon, Stashu and himself. The three men had been separated from their own companies, cut off and surrounded. They were outnumbered by what seemed like the entire Red Army against the population of a Polish backwater village.

"The Ruskis will soon be all over us like flies on a dead horse." Stashu, often the crazy one, continued, "We're dead. Only one chance: surrender, then escape. Follow me..."

Andrzej recalled that the three of them abandoned their dugout and did just that, without question.

Often the Russian soldiers serving on guard duty were untrained and lacked adequate support. It was a job no one wanted. Long nights were spent hanging around in sub-zero temperatures. The prisoners had been stripped of their weapons but somehow Stashu had managed to get a bottle of Polish Spirit and secreted it in his coat. He offered the bottle to the guard in exchange for a Russian roll-up. Although the Russian soldier could just have taken the liquor, he seemed to go along with the offer as if he had felt somehow in control of the situation.

Gods knows what was in the bottle. Stashu thought it had smelled as if it should have been used to "preserve a wooden s***hole" but the two young guards passed it between them. In no time it had thawed them through. Within the hour they were both legless.

"Come on, now we go," said Stashu. "We can pick up arms on the way – loads lying around."

"The Great Escape" had been related on many occasions by Stashu. It always ended in the three of them rolling around in laughter. Each time the tale of the escape was told, it was bigger, more dangerous, more daring, and after a while it was unrecognisable. Andrzej and Leon never joined in, as they had completely forgotten just how much the truth had been stretched and the story had been embellished.

The three of them had defied death so many times and this was no joke. Many times in the fields, then once by surrendering and escaping, but fate had now caught up with Leon and his luck had run out.

Andrzej could not allow himself to dwell on this too much or he could lose focus and share his friend's fate. But how could he let go of the friend with whom he'd shared such extremes of experience? He had to calm down and stay sharp. But try as he might, this tragedy was to stay with him and serve as the death-knell of his youth.

Back around the fire, the remainder of the group made attempts at jovial but respectful humour, acknowledging the loss of a good man. Eventually, they broke away to be with their own thoughts that drifted to their loved ones and to Leon's family who did not even know of their loss.

Andrzej thought of Anka, who had been the most important part of Leon's dreams of a future and whose photograph he had carried in his wallet, close to his heart. She had given it to him on only their third meeting, just over two years ago now: a picture of her standing, smiling, wearing the chequered headscarf and her immaculate, long, white apron.

Most of the men had been brought up in strict Catholic families and still practised their faith. So it was no surprise that, later that evening when they had bedded-down in an old disused church, many of them could be seen, lips moving silently, crucifix in hand. Their prayers were aided by the lingering aroma of incense that permeated every pew.

Andrzej spent another troubled night, unable to sleep and smoking too much. He got up at first light and scraped some of the mud from his boots. Morning came quickly with light piercing through cracks in the stained-glass windows; piercing too was Andrzej's whistling of a patriotic song.

Men, still half asleep, shunned the rules of rank and called out: "Pack it in, Gwizdak!" and "What the hell time do you call this?"

Commanders and leaders now rallied the men with determination and unswerving control. It was yet another day in the field for these war-weary men, but the battle cries reverberated with renewed vigour.

"Push on! You owe it to your fallen comrades to give them all the glory you can for their sacrifice. They have died for Poland, now we must strive and battle on to ensure their beloved homeland is not lost forever!"

At the end of one fervent speech, some of the troops could be heard as they moved forward.

"This one's for you, Stanczak."

"I'll get the bastards back for you, Zyskowski."

In the days to come, there was more of the same from the higher-ranking officers, as if to compel their men to victory. "We must all push ourselves to our extreme limits of endurance and then beyond. Hear me: we shall be victorious.

Losing is not an option."

"When you have given all you have to give – give more. This is the only way we shall get through this and we will. Poland's existence depends on you."

The men emerged from what seemed like an endless barrage to catch sight of a young soldier. He looked barely eighteen and they saw that he was having great difficulty trying to crawl across the field in front of their line.

Andrzej raised his arm. "Hold your fire, he's one of ours."

"Sarge, it's Kazmierski. He's been missing."

They quickly assessed that he was wounded. On command, two men broke rank, dropped to the ground and began to crawl forward through the mud and thick smoke to their young comrade. They stopped periodically with ears close to the ground, waiting for a break in sniper fire and then, under cover from their own men, proceeded forward again. As they again emerged from another battering, they saw that Kazmierski was trying to get up. He tried to prop himself up on the butt of his rifle but fell down again. The men shouted, "Stay low. Keep your head down." Then they saw the jagged bone protruding from his shortened leg, strips of skin and ripped tendons dangling from torn muscle.

When the men reached him, he was still clutching his severed foot, as if he could not bear to leave part of himself behind.

"Oh Jesu. Mama, Mama." As the young soldier cried out for his mother, the older men comforted him.

"Come on son, don't cry, you'll be all right now. Just hang on."

One of the men grabbed the blood-drenched boot and its contents and hurled it as far as he could as they proceeded to drag him to safety.

A few days later, the men asked the medical orderly how the lad was doing.

"He's upset about his boots. He'd just got them. He said

he knew his days of fighting were over the second he lost his foot. Anyway, he reckons one boot is no good to anyone. He didn't want to go home with nothing to show for it and he wanted to give the boots to his younger brother. He says he had never had any boots or shoes of his own, only his sister's old cast-offs."

Meanwhile, Andrzej and his men were sacking the depleted stock of a nearby ammunition dump. Their equipment was mostly made up of First World War remnants. Guns had been manufactured in different countries and therefore required separate bullets. Things were dire. As the men went through the boxes, discarding one and picking up the next, their frustration began to bite.

"Oh Christ, this is bloody impossible. Trying to find the right bullets is like sending a blind man to pick mushrooms. I'm going to have to ditch this Mosin. Best sniper rifle yet, but no ammo." Bogdan Downarowicz had a keen eye.

"How come you're such a good shot, Bogdan?" asked Andrzej, who had noted that his new comrade had the best aim he had ever seen.

"My father used to take us hunting. That is, my brothers and me. Catching rabbits in the old forests near Minsk. We used to get the odd wild boar sometimes, as well."

"Were your brothers good shots?"

"Oh, hell no. The old man used to say they couldn't hit a bison if it was tied to a tree. No patience. They couldn't sit still long enough and wait like me." Bogdan picked up one gun after another, inspecting them and holding them to his shoulder and aiming them at an imaginary target.

"This will be okay. French rifles are not as good as Russian ones. Heavier, you know. But then there's plenty of ammo for it and it's got a good sight. It'll have to do."

The men had to leave with only meagre supplies.

Out of nowhere, a heavy storm struck up. Andrzej and Bodgan, along with their company, moved fast. They ran through a field, scrambled down a muddy embankment and crossed a stream to find shelter in a large, corrugated tin hut. The wind and rain howled outside. The respite from the blast gave them a surreal feeling of protection as the weather thundered on the tin roof.

"Strange weather for August," said one man.

"It could be an omen," said a pale-looking young man.

"Omen, shnomen, what the hell does that mean?" said Bogdan.

Sweating and steaming, the men now sat calmly and thoughtfully as they prepared themselves for the next few days.

"We move forward towards Warsaw tomorrow. It's the last push. It's going to be hellish tough," said Andrzej.

"It's now or never. And we can't afford to lose," said Bogdan.

"This will be the Armageddon of our campaign," said an older soldier with greying hair and an educated voice.

"The sky is weeping for Poland," said the pale-looking young man.

"What crap," said Bogdan. "You're defeated before you start".

Andrzej, turned away and spoke quietly to Bogdan "The lad's terrified, we need to watch out for him". He then addressed all the men. "The tactical advantage is that the Red Army will have to drag all their stuff through deep mud. Their vehicles have a shorter track than ours and they will get bogged down," said Andrzej. "We're pretty much sorted, just waiting for them to come within range. Now, have you got that?"

"Yes, Sarge. Sorry, Sarge," said the pale young soldier.

August 1921: outskirts of Warsaw

The Polish army was poised and ready to fight to the bitter end. Shortly before the battle commenced, the men were gathered together for their final instructions.

"This is it, men. Before you go in, I am here to report to you that Premier Wincenty Witos has announced today that any soldiers who fought on the front line in the Great War and who serve on the front line again today will not only receive medals for their bravery but, following our victory, will receive lands free of charge. God be with you all. Raise the White Eagle and don't let him waver."

Back in the field, the Russians greatly outnumbered the Polish Army and the task at times seemed hopeless, even absurd. Incredibly, as the days progressed, the Russians began to lose ground. There was no let up from the Poles and, to the amazement of the Russian Army, they realised they were being pushed back.

With unprecedented faith and ferocity, the Poles fought on, driving their aggressor to defeat. The outcome was as much a shock to the Poles as to the Russians, and came to be known by the proud victors as "The Miracle at the Vistula." In actuality, the miracle was wrought by the Poles themselves, comprising of a phenomenal push from the beleaguered Reserve Army, a risky strategy from Marshal Jozef Pilsudski, and vital knowledge from the cryptographers who had cracked the Red Army radio codes.

Pilsudski quickly became the nation's hero, the focus of the country's pride, as Poland was re-born yet again.

3. POLAND 1921

Nowa Wola

Andrzej was in his quarters in an old farmhouse, collecting his belongings and packing his bags. He was leaving the army for what he hoped was the last time. He looked at a photograph of himself in uniform, taken the previous September in a northern Polish town on the outskirts of Warsaw. He turned the picture over and saw what he had written on the back: Nowa Wola 10 1X 1920. The picture had been taken following the battle for Warsaw.

"What a hell of a fight that was." Andrzej said to himself.

Following the victory, Andrzej Gwizdak and a selected number of his brothers-in-arms were commended as members of an acclaimed group regarded as Poland's most loyal and staunch defenders. After fighting bravely and selflessly on the front line in two wars, their reward was an allotment of land adjoining the Russian border. The land was chosen to create a buffer zone to prevent any further infringement from the Russian military.

Andrzej and over fifty of his comrades were each allotted land to build farms and homesteads in the area of Nowogrodek in northeast Poland.

Premier Witos had also declared that any volunteers who had fought on the front line in the recent war would also be entitled to purchase plots adjoining the Russian border. Fifty-nine more settlements (osadas) were created in this area and many more were planned, stretching south, all along the Polish/Russian border.

Andrzej's regiment had been demobilised near the town of Maladzecna and he was fortunate enough to be invited to stay with his friend, Bogdan Downarowicz, whose family resided in the area. Bogdan had four brothers, Mieczyslaw, Antoni, Wincenty and Jozef, all of whom were military men; this was compulsory at the time, irrespective of a person's social or educational status.

For the first time in what seemed like forever, Andrzej was slowly becoming acquainted to a life away from the battlefield and the sole company of other soldiers.

Bogdan was staying with his mother and three sisters, Stanislawa "Stasha", Helena and Andzia. Stasha was the eldest at twenty-two.

Life at home was a busy, noisy affair with everyone trying to assert their influence on events, discussions and plans. As in many Polish families, everyone was sure that he or she knew best. To an outsider, these family interactions seemed like ongoing squabbles that complicated everything. To the family members themselves, it was simple: life was not worth a zloty if it was not lived with power, zest and passion.

It was Sunday afternoon and the whole family and a few friends, including Andrzej, had converged on the Downarowicz household. A large joint of pork had been slowly sizzling while they attended the local Catholic Church for early Sunday Mass. The smell was mouth-wateringly good, and everyone was loudly commenting on this and their attendant hunger.

Mama and the three girls busied themselves between the stove and the kitchen table, stirring gravy, mashing potatoes and dishing up vegetables. There was a clanging of pans and utensils and much chattering. The men did not cook at all and, to be honest, the women could not cope with them anywhere near the food preparation. Many a man had nearly lost his fingers, sneaking up and pinching bits of raw carrot and the like from the chopping board.

Stasha turned to her younger brother. "If you want to make yourself useful, Wincenty, put another log on the fire."

As the food was being served up, there was a sudden commotion at the table. Mieczyslaw, "Mietek", the eldest son, had just entered the room:

"Oi, yoi, yoi, I don't believe what I see. Who asked you to do this? Since we buried father, I am the eldest and head of the family. He is the youngest and he has just started to carve the roast." An older brother would often take offence if a younger sibling did the slightest thing to challenge his position in the family.

"Brother, ignore him, he makes a mistake, huh?"

"Don't you tell me what to do. Who does he think he is? Where is his respect?"

"Mietek, just leave it."

"No, he must apologise."

"But you were late, we thought you weren't coming."

"I wasn't late, you started dinner too early."

"You should have come home sooner."

"Don't you tell me what to do! I come when I want. I'm the head of the family."

Then Mama intervened. "Quiet, all of you. Stop bickering and sit down for your dinner. We've not spent hours in the kitchen to watch the dinner ruin while you all argue. You are spoiling my appetite. Mietek, as you are the oldest and head of the family, please say grace and then we can start before it all gets cold." No one challenged Mama and peace reigned for a while.

While parents could be very strict, they did not see a need for reserve so gatherings of family and friends were characterised by high spirits and an unchecked desire to have fun: singing, dancing and laughing. People were judged on their manners, common sense, hard work and Catholic values. There was trouble only when someone got cocky or when too much vodka had been flowing or, worse still, both.

It was in this atmosphere that Andrzej and his friends began to rebuild their lives. The young soldiers and local young women had taken to meeting regularly and these interactions had replaced gunfire in making their adrenalin flow. Andrzej, Bogdan and his four brothers and three sisters were all part of this social maelstrom.

Stasha had liked Andrzej from the minute she met him. It was not difficult to find him attractive as he was strong, confident and spoke well in company. He was also much admired by his friends because of his reputation as a soldier. He knew what he wanted and his actions spoke louder than words, as he was already a driving force behind the planning of the new settlement. A committee of men now met daily to discuss the building requirements of their proposed community.

Stasha was no fool. She was practical and capable. A devout Catholic, she was not fanatical but fervent in her commitment to honesty and decency. She knew she was an attractive girl, slim with long, dark hair. However, she had suffered smallpox as a child, which had left her with a little scarring on her face. She was conscious of it, shy, and though she used make-up to cover the marks, she was less sure of herself than other girls.

Stasha would not push herself forward in company and when she met Andrzej socially, she probably gave the impression that she had no interest in him. She steered clear of any chance of rejection and the awkward and embarrassing situations this could lead to. So she confined herself to watching him from a distance.

Andrzej was popular with the girls and Stasha noticed how easily they would approach and flirt with him. However, Andrzej was also proud and stubborn and when he saw a girl flit from one man to another, he no longer took her seriously.

Saturday evening arrived and it seemed like the whole area

had turned out for the local dance. Stasha was talking to her brother Bogdan, when Andrzej approached.

"I don't often see you dance, Stasha. Are you waiting for someone special?"

She knew he was only joking but she was embarrassed as it was true.

"It's a polka. How about it, Stasha? While you're waiting for your prince, we can give it a try if you'll risk some broken toes."

Stasha was getting used to his way of never letting his guard down, eschewing romance even as he asked her to dance with him.

He led her to the floor. His hands were big and strong and he noted in comparison how soft hers were, with unusually long, slender fingers. As he took hold of her waist he noticed that he could almost encircle it with one hand. In only a few moments he realised that he was assessing this young woman's attributes in a way that he had never done before. Hers were diligent hands and she had a body that did not lend itself to overeating and lethargy. He admired her very much.

Andrzej also noted how her long dark hair, held back with combs at each side, had an intense shine. Stasha had always worn her hair tied up when Andrzej had seen her before. Now, with her wavy hair flowing free, she looked younger and more carefree. She smelled lovely too.

"I like your scent, Stasha."

"Oh, do you? It's honeysuckle."

Andrzej recalled how the plant had grown all along the picket fence of his house back home. When he had slammed the gate shut, the scent would catch the air.

What a stark contrast to his months of fighting, eating and sleeping with his comrades, when taking a bath has been a rare luxury. They had all become used to a sweaty, musty smell. Now, with his nose next to Stasha's ear, she was intoxicating to him.

The hall was crowded with soldiers and local people. Everyone seemed to be there and there was no room to move. So they just danced on the spot and Stasha found it easier to chat with the crowd to shield them from eavesdroppers.

"Bogdan tells me that you are involved with building a new township near the Russian border." Stasha attempted polite conversation with Andrzej, but she was more interested in finding out what he was planning to do with his future.

"Yes, that's right. I'll be leaving soon and the house building is to start as soon as possible. My brother Frank is coming up from the south to join us. He's a carpenter and joiner and we need his skills. The houses are to be chalet-style. First off, we go to cut the wood from the Naliboka forest just northeast of Nowogrodek. Last week, we picked up quite a few ex-military horses. Some will do as work-horses and the rest we will use for breeding," said Andrzej.

"It must be an exciting project, planning and building a village from scratch."

"Certainly is. We are all anxious to get started. We have been like nomads for the last few years and it will be good to have a permanent base. You must come and see us, Stasha. Come with Bogdan. It's not too far away. We could probably do with a woman's opinion on some of the planning, like the requirements for the interiors of the houses."

Later that evening, Stasha reflected on the night and told herself that she must not read too much into one dance and a little conversation, as he was a friend of her brother and was perhaps only being polite.

A week later, Andrzej moved away from Maladzecna, in the district of Minsk, where Stasha lived with her family. He joined the rest of the men and the felling of trees commenced. Frank arrived and they worked together in teams. The plan was to construct individual farmhouses, barns and outhouses. Their settlement was to be known as

Osada Puzieniewicze.

It was a tough time. Over the next few months, the men had to live in very basic, makeshift camps of dugouts and lean-tos and it was all much harder and more exhausting than any of them had anticipated. The reliability of food and other supply deliveries was poor and spasmodic. Some men found it too much and gave up and left.

The die-hards continued and eventually the day dawned when the basics were almost complete. Andrzej took a well-earned break and was invited to the Downarowicz's family home to celebrate a Holy Day. Although Andrzej did not share the religious fervour of his hosts, he went along with it all for the sake of his friend and the heady and surprising new interest he had in his friend's sister.

Stasha had missed Andrzej more than she had expected and this made her feel even more awkward now he was here for a visit. Bogdan noticed that Stasha looked uncomfortable and followed her outside the house.

"Is something bothering you, Stasha?"

"Oh no, it was just a little stuffy inside, so I thought I'd get some fresh air."

"Are you upset that Andrzej is here? He seems to think that you are avoiding him."

"No, not at all. I just don't know what to say to him," replied Stasha.

Bogdan wondered whether he should say anything and then thought: oh, why not. "He likes you a lot, you know. He told me and he says he is going to ask you to go with him to the social after Sunday mass."

A few more months passed and Stasha and Andrzej had managed to meet up a couple more times. Andrzej took a break from his building project and came to stay with Stasha's family again for a few days.

"Stasha, you look lovely," was the response from the womenfolk as she entered the room wearing a new dress.

Mama was beaming and her sisters were very proud of the creation. Stasha had sought their opinions during the design and finishing; all the women in her family were adept at sewing. Other female friends had joined them for tea and they instantly gathered round, talking ten to the dozen.

"Where did you get the fabric from? It's quite exquisite." Bronka, Bodgan's girlfriend, was smitten. "Can you help me to make something similar? It's wonderful."

Feeling a little overpowered with all the attention, Stasha replied quietly, "We have recently exchanged our sewing machine for a better model. Now I can do more intricate work." She continued more confidently, "This is the fabric I bought from a Jewish man who had a stall at the market in the square. I'd never seen him there before."

"Oh, I know who you mean. He is there every week now. He has some lovely things. Did you buy the lace from him also?"

"No, Mama gave me the lace for my Saint's Day gift. She bought it from a neighbour. It's hand-made and quite old. I bleached it and it came up really well."

Then her youngest sister, Andzia, declared, "It's so lovely. You could get married in a dress like that." Stasha's face was burning.

Andrzej had just entered the room and heard the comment; he quickly took Stasha's hand and led her out into the garden.

"Let's cool off before we go," said Andrzej. Stasha noticed that he was behaving very oddly and was in quite a silly mood.

"Why don't you go and change into something else, Stasha?"

Her face dropped. "What's wrong with this? Don't you think it suits me, Andrzej?" Stasha felt deflated and downcast as she tentatively smoothed the skirt and then straightened the sleeves in turn. "And I felt so pleased with it."

Like most men, Andrzej could not remember a single

thing that Stasha had ever worn in the past, but he said, "That dress you wore last time I was here was nice and you looked good in it. Why don't you save your new one and consider whether you might wear it as a wedding dress?"

"What do you mean?" Stasha paused for a minute and then continued with uncharacteristic boldness, "Am I to suppose that you are asking me to marry you?" For a moment, she panicked and wondered if she had misunderstood. Andrzej just nodded.

"Oh, really Andrzej," said Stasha, smiling and prodding him. "What sort of proposal is that?"

"The only one you'll get from me. I am a soldier, not a matinee idol."

They laughed and stood there for a minute or two with their foreheads together, feeling a bit giddy. He kissed her briefly. He was feeling awkward and thought that someone could be watching them. Then, as they held each other's gaze, they began to consider the enormity of the challenge before them.

Andrzej had had one or two girlfriends before, but this was serious. This woman was to be his wife and the mother of his children. They had a lot of work to do together but he knew Stasha would toil just as hard as he would to make a success of it.

"Life will not be easy, Stash. We will have to learn new farming skills and be self-sufficient. It will be hard graft, so what I have to offer is no bed of roses."

"I'm ready to face any challenge to be with you and I don't care what it takes. I don't shrink from getting my hands dirty." Stasha was happy to go along with whatever life had to offer but she was also sensible and realised it would probably be much tougher than she could now guess.

They strolled back to the house, hand in hand. "We think the dress is a great success but Stasha has decided to save it for a wedding." Complete silence followed his remark as no one was sure what it meant.

"Mamma, Andrzej has asked me to marry him and I have accepted. I hope this has the blessing of the whole family." Stasha knew that everyone would be pleased, nobody more so than Bogdan.

"I could not wish for more. My best friend is to marry my sister. Excellent. This calls for a toast. We need vodka."

Mama's beaming smile swiftly evaporated. "Not before church."

"Just one little one, Mama. It's a very special occasion."

"Well, go on then, just this once. A small one, mind you. I know you boys all too well, so wait until afterwards to do the real celebrating. I shall be ashamed if you are worse for wear in church and..."

Mama's voice was drowned out by general laughter and chatter, as the men reached for glasses and a rather large flagon. Bogdan had taken to brewing illicit vodka, a practice ostensibly frowned upon by the local priest. He had got wind of what was going on when the family's chickens were seen running round in circles in the middle of the road in a drunken stupor, squawking wildly, after Bogdan had fed them with some of his brewing dregs.

Now, no more was said about it, except that the priest visited the Downarowicz household more frequently and always left with a tell-tale package wrapped in brown paper. This quickly became a family joke, repeated whenever Bogdan brought out his home-brew. It always evoked the same laughter as if they were hearing it for the first time. In a way this was the case, as this was to become yet another story that would be exaggerated and embellished as time went by.

Andrzej had to return to his village construction site. The couple hastily discussed and planned their future. They knew that hard work lay ahead of them but they were more than prepared for the challenge. Andrzej knew that Stasha was the only woman he had ever met who would be prepared, with total commitment and devotion, to help him build a life out of nothing. She would be his friend, his lover and his partner.

4. PUZIENIEWICZE 1928

Life was settled, work on the land was hard but rewarding and there was peace in Europe. Over the past few years, Stasha and Andrzej had given their all, as had the friends and neighbours who formed their new community.

Much of the land allotted to the settlers had been war-torn and neglected and had demanded sheer hard graft to make it arable and suitable for grazing and raising livestock.

They had all suffered in the years when crops failed, horses had fallen sick and could not work and the thatched-roofed houses had caught fire. Yet, through all of this, helping one another where they could, they had succeeded and come through with a sense of great satisfaction.

This was so for the Gwizdak family. The once bleak expanse of land was now their farm, their home and their very own inalienable territory.

You would often hear Andrzej before you could see him as he had a familial peculiarity, a habit of expressing the music going around his head through pursed lips. For those who do not find comfort in this odd practice, whistling can be very irritating. However, his ability to do so strongly and tunefully created a certain amount of acceptance.

It was a typical late summer's day in this strip of northeast Europe, trapped beneath Lithuania and above the impassable boggy Pripet marshes to the south. The colours of the land, nature's own kaleidoscope of shades of green, brown and gold, shone strong and bright against a clear blue sky and there was a pleasing smell of warm earth.

Row after row of wheat-sheaves stood to attention in perfect symmetry, like an army declaring that the battle of their own field was won. A gentle breeze stirred the remaining fields of corn and barley, wafting a hint of clover in the air, giving the promise of honey.

Andrzej hammered the last fence post home and stood back to check that it was straight. He placed the mallet back in his tool bag. A job well done. As he set off for home, he looked up at the stork nesting on the chimneystack of the beekeeper's house. They reckoned it was supposed to bring fertility. Well, it didn't work here, did it? No children. I'm not surprised though, thought Andrzej, he's so feckless. Anyway, babies don't come from playing with bees. Nothing to do with fertility at all, the stork only nests there because they put an old cartwheel on top of the stack. Well, that's one way to block a chimney.

He stopped at the gate and passed a minute or two with the beekeeper, one of his closest neighbours. "Hi Jozef. How's it going? Do you have problems with smoke on account of that nest on your chimney?"

"Oh, hello, Andrzej. Well actually, the other day, there was smoke billowing out everywhere and this smoked some of the bees out of their hives. Never happened before. We had swarms all over, bees all over the house."

Andrzej muttered under his breath, "Most excitement you must have had in months."

The beekeeper's wife Zofia was blonde, buxom and quite a head-turner in the village. She also had a tendency to flirt with every man she encountered. However, her husband never noticed any of this and was such a clown. Everyone wondered how they had ever got together. Andrzej pondered: surely, nobody could possibly like honey that much?

As he took his leave and started to walk down the lane towards his own farm, his neighbour called after him, "Andrzej, are you going into Mir next week?"

"Yes, Tuesday, I am going to the miller's. I have arranged to pay him extra to mill the grain early. He is very busy but I want to catch the markets for a good price."

"Can Zofia travel with you? She needs to drop off the honey in time for the market."

"Okay, but tell her I may be a while. I have a lot of business to attend to. If she is happy to wait, then she can come along. Tell her, Tuesday."

As he walked past a ramshackle wooden house and outbuildings bordering on his land, Andrzej wondered how long this elderly neighbour could continue. As a widower and childless man, he was alone with his arthritic bones, without help to bring in a harvest or plough a field. This man had lived on his land long before Andrzej and his fellow settlers had arrived. He had befriended the old man and had given him help and support when he was struggling, as did others in the village.

There was an understanding that one day in the future Andrzej would make him an offer for these extra twenty hectares. This would bring the size of the Gwizdak's farm to just over forty-five hectares. Funds were accumulating nicely in the Co-operative Bank in the nearby town of Mir. Things were looking good.

An air of anticipated celebration vibrated throughout the village as, come the next weekend, a great social event was being arranged. Although the weather was freezing cold, a ceremony was to take place outside. Living through these winters, where temperatures were mostly sub-zero, the people of Puzieniewicze had become a tough lot. Many chores still had to be done outside, freezing or not.

As most of the couples had married around the same

time, children were also of a similar age, mostly five and under.

Andrzej and Stasha's first-born, Jozef, had arrived after just one year, followed by a daughter, Janina the year after, then their second son, Benedykt (Benek) and the latest, a baby boy, Mieczyslaw (Mietek).

The children from the village had never had a big communal bonfire before and there was immense excitement. The men of the village did not share their enthusiasm and were quite solemn. To them it was a remembrance day as well as a celebration. The burning pine logs did nothing to lift their spirits either as the smell haunted them all; reminding them of the terrible fields of slaughter in two wars which seemed much less than ten and eight years ago.

Potatoes were roasting around the edge of the fire.

"Can I have mine now, Mama?" Said Jozef.

"We've only just put them on the fire Jozef. They won't be cooked yet"

"How long will it be?" Young Jozef was not one to wait for anything

"Is it ready now Mamma?"

"No my son, you must wait a little longer."

A minute later "Is it ready now?"

"Not quite, I will tell you when?"

"Is it 'when' yet Mama?"

This continued every minute. In the end Jozef ate a half-cooked potato, but the look on his face was a picture as if it was the most delicious thing he had ever eaten; Jozef called it "my potato in its uniform". This set the precedence and as soon as the other children saw Jozef with his potato they all had to eat half-cooked potatoes.

Janina, who was only four years old but quite practical, spat it out and was not impressed.

The parents put more on the embers by the fire and when they were properly cooked, the children tasted fluffy potatoes with lashings of their own village butter.

Stasha had to blow on Benek's to prevent him from burning his mouth, as he stamped his feet impatiently because he wanted to hold it himself like his elder brother and sister.

Then came the moment they had all been waiting for. With much ceremony, the local priest headed a procession followed by local musicians and four men from the village carried a three metre high wooden cross bearing a plaque that said:

1918-1928

This cross was erected by the Osadnicy in memory of the 10th anniversary of Poland's independence Puzieniewicze 11th day of November 1928.

Andrzej and Stasha had now been married for seven years and there were already five little Gwizdaks. Another baby son, Czeslaw (Cheshek) had joined the brood six months before. The beekeeper and his wife were still childless.

Stasha confronted Andrzej. "I think I might be pregnant again. It certainly would be easier if I had just a bit more time between the children. I am now seriously thinking of putting a cartwheel on our chimney."

"Stasha, you say yourself that our children are God's blessing. We are doing well. Perhaps we should think about hiring more help. That would make things a little easier for you." They were both very tired. "The harvest is in now and I think we could take a little time to relax," said Andrzej.

They were in their barn, talking, while he soaped a saddle lying across a homemade wooden horse. Stasha was sitting on a bale of straw, baby Cheshek was napping and this was one of her very few stolen moments of peace.

"The children will soon be able to do jobs like this. They are already picking vegetables and collecting eggs. I think we should start showing Jozef and Janina how to go on," said Stasha.

"Yes, that way, they can earn their pocket money," said Andrzej.

Milking was now done three times a day, as well as a hundred and one other chores. They were also part of the cheese production co-operative, which was flourishing. If it continued as it was, there would be an opening in the future to export their surplus, creating new trading potential. Being part of the agricultural group and co-operative meant that they could share the larger farm machinery and use it as they required it. They had a rota for maintenance and for housing to prevent machinery rusting through the long and extremely cold winters.

They now had a variety of healthy livestock, acres of different grains and they were virtually self-sufficient. Their neighbours were also in good situations; some were slightly better off than others but in general their community was a real success story.

Winter was now closing in and the harvest was complete. Andrzej had paid the miller even more than usual this year to get his grains milled early but it had been worth it. The surplus had been sold off, mostly to the Jewish community in nearby Mir, and their own stores had been well stocked.

Meats had been smoked and salted and sausage had been made from off-cuts. Cabbage had been stored in wooden barrels with layers of salt, onions strung, potatoes and vegetables packed and stored and fruits preserved. The larder had been completely replenished. Looking around, they decided to invite Stasha's family to visit.

They had just turned in for the night. Andrzej rolled a cigarette. "Andrzej, why do you have to smoke that thing in bed?" Stasha was not happy about him smoking as much as he did. "I am getting to the point where I am embarrassed to hang my sheets on the washing-line. They are full of holes. You fall asleep with that thing in your mouth and I fear that one of these days the house will burn down while we are all in our beds."

"Stop whinging, woman. I fall asleep because I am dog-tired."

Stasha kept quiet. She knew that arguing was a waste of time and energy. After all, everyone knew that only men got really tired. She blamed him for her insomnia, not only because she was so often heavily pregnant but because she lived in fear of the bed catching fire and so stayed awake until he had put out his roll-up.

"At least there is one saving grace: with a roll-up in your mouth, you can't whistle." She propped herself up, pummelled her pillow and turned over.

"Women. You always have to have the last word," replied Andrzej.

Stasha thought to herself: no we don't. Men always have the last word by saying just that.

Over the next few days, they discussed their plans for a family visit.

"We'll kill another pig then," said Andrzej.

"My family has a voracious appetite, and there are now so many of them, but that should do the job," said Stasha. "And it will probably be better if we wait for the first snow. They'll be much more comfortable travelling on sleighs than the rough roads or thick mud."

"Good idea, Stasha, so be it."

The children could not remember their mother's family visiting en-masse before and they were very excited. The planning had been going on for a week. Uncle Bogdan and Aunt Bronka and their cousin Klara lived a few kilometres away and were the only family they saw regularly. Uncle Bodgan made something that only grown-ups could drink but they mustn't talk about it; it was a secret. They had heard Tata tell Mama that Uncle Bogdan was making more than usual for the family party.

"Stasha, shall I take the pig's feet?" Aunt Bronka,

Bogdan's wife, had come to help out.

"Oh thanks, Bron. You make the best salceson." Her sister-in-law would simmer the pig's feet with vegetables and add the sweet pork near to the bone. The brawn would then be turned out of its mould and served on a large platter. Even the babies would be fed a portion of this.

A huge pan of bigos (salted, fermented cabbage cooked with meats) was stewing and would be served with slices of sourdough rye bread for everyone to tuck into when they arrived.

"I've made a large batch of cream cheese and they can all have this and lard spread for starters," said Stasha, wiping her forehead. "My neighbour, Danuta Slowaski, has offered to bake extra bread, so that will be a big help."

Bronka stood at Stasha's kitchen table, helping to prepare salted herrings for pickling. "Your lard spread is the best, Stasha. I don't know how you get the crackling so crispy. I try but it is never like yours."

"Of course it is, you're too critical of yourself. Shall I put chopped, pickled dill cucumbers in the potato salad or should I just add onions and dill weed? What do you think?" The women were enjoying their companionable afternoon in the kitchen.

"I wish preparing the family meal every day was as pleasant as this."

"I know. I've had a lovely day. Thanks for all your help, Bronka. It was so good of Bogdan to come as well, to help Andrzej. I wouldn't have had time to do all the preparation as well as my other chores."

"I'll bake a cheesecake as I promised, and perhaps a poppy-seed roll, since you are making the plum pie and babki cake."

"That would be good of you. Now let's have that lemon tea. We've earned it." Stasha reached for the teapot, part of her wedding gift from her sisters. She very nearly dropped it as the children ran in, around her feet.

"Can we have some...?"

"No, no. Always, can we have? Go and wash your hands and come back in ten minutes at least. Aunt Bronka and I want peace and quiet to drink our tea."

"How long is ten minutes, mamma?" asked Benek.

"As long as it takes you to wash your hands ten times."

"Oh, come on Janka, I don't want to wash my hands anyway."

Jozef grabbed a jug, drank milk directly from it and promptly got rapped round his ears with a tea towel. Jozef, Janina and Benek dashed off into the family room. The children were often very restless at this time of year, as temperatures were below zero and it was too cold to play outside.

"Keep your eye on Mietek and play with him," said Stasha.

The women drank their tea and planned the rest of the weekend visit.

"To start, we will have soup." This was made with dried mushrooms, stock, cream and garlic. The children had been going to the forest with the grown-ups from an early age to learn to recognise and pick the mushrooms. As it was now winter, the mushrooms had been dried and strung in long garlands and stored in the larder. Stasha reflected that once summer came, the children would also pick sorrel to make another delicious soup with a sweet and sour flavour.

"And then to follow: how shall we cook the pork?"

Bronka said, "Everyone likes golabki."

Uncle Bogdan was the first to arrive with his accordion and a couple of large flagons.

"How strong is it this time, Bogdan? I'm just wondering how much of this cherry juice to add." Andrzej took the first large jug and mixed the vodka with the juice, to produce a drink called Wisniowka.

"Don't drown it. We want to taste the fire, not a weak

cordial."

"Bogdan, you are used to drinking it strong. When anyone else tries it, it nearly blows their head off. I am going to add a bit more. It will go further."

The children would be given just a little taste, although Jozef usually tried to coax more out of Uncle Bogdan.

"You must let the boys have a little sip, Andrzej. Then alcohol will not hold any mystery for them," said Bogdan. "If all children were allowed a taste they would not grow up thinking that they must drink because all adults do. That's what my parents did."

"I see. Did it work, then?" asked Andrzej.

"Er, well – no," said Bogdan.

"Thought not. Not only do you drink copious amounts of the stuff, you now almost have you own private distillery", said Andrzej.

At this Bogdan howled with laughter and Andrzej joined him.

"You're only jealous 'cos you can't take drink like me, ha ha," said Bogdan.

He was right. Andrzej would only take a little amount of alcohol. His side of the family had always suffered from stomach problems and too much gave him bad heartburn. Just as well, thought Andrzej. Daily farm chores did not go away just because a farmer had a hangover.

Andrzej gave Bogdan some leeway with his sons. Bogdan really loved his nephews and would have liked a son of his own. However, after the difficult birth of their only child, their daughter Klara, there would be no more.

The snow was falling quite heavily and the rest of Stasha's family arrived on horse-drawn sleighs. Andrzej and Bogdan were waiting, ready to help. They lifted Babka down first and Bogdan took his mother's arm and led her into the house. Andrzej and his brothers-in-law lifted the rest of the women and children down from the sleighs.

They removed the fur rugs, shook off the snow and took

them to the barn. The women were already chattering and collecting the contributions they had brought with them. They walked to the porch of the house and everyone was falling over each other as they struggled to remove their snow-covered boots.

"Come back here and shake the snow from your hat." The children could not wait to see their cousins.

"Hello, hello, so lovely to see you." There were kisses, hugs, back patting and then the usual tears. "Oh, so good. We are one big family again."

They walked through the hall where everyone dipped and made a sign as they passed a picture of the Virgin and Child and a large crucifix hanging on the wall.

Stasha smiled and gestured, "Come on in and make yourself comfortable. Our home is your home." Everyone was talking at once. Chatting and laughter competed with the noise of children running around.

"Oh my. Janina and Benedykt, how you have grown." Stasha's mother was taken through to the family room first. "Now, where is Jozef? Come here and kiss babka."

Jozef hung back and as his grandmother briefly looked away, he pulled a face. He received a playful tap on the back of the head from his mother as she pushed him forward.

"Mama, let me take your coat." Stasha showed her mother to a large, comfortable chair near the fire. Mietek needed no prompting and held out his arms, kissed his babka and sat at her feet. Stasha's mother then reached out and, without words, exchanged her coat for baby Cheshek. Stasha's mother snuggled her youngest grandson in her arms, the picture of contentment and happiness.

To everyone's amusement, she said, "Oh, why can't we women have grandchildren first?"

Stasha announced, "Andrzej and the men will join us soon. They are just seeing to the horses."

The men came in and there was lots more kissing, hugging and backslapping. Babka spoke out, "I thank God for this, all together, and everybody well. It makes me so happy." She wiped away a tear with a lace-edged handkerchief that wafted a hint of lavender as she replaced it in the pocket of her skirt.

They settled down in the large family room where an open log fire was blazing away, cracking and spitting. The warmth was complemented by the wonderful smell of pine. Their chalet-style house had a dry, warm smell in summer but in the winter months a more pronounced, clean, resinous scent.

The children ran out and took their cousins to their bedrooms to "show them our things" and "find things to play with".

As soon as they heard the word "vodka", the men followed Bogdan like sheep and he wasted no time in pouring out large measures of his "best stuff yet".

The women chatted and admired Stasha's home. The traditional heavy wooden furniture had been softened with big feather cushions that Stasha had made herself a few years before.

"I remember thinking at the time, how do I manage to do all this with two children?" said Stasha. "Now I have five."

"I am surprised we manage to get everything done," said one of her sisters-in-law. The women all acknowledged this. Their status as Catholic wives meant that ever-increasing families were taken for granted.

Embroidered table covers and antimacassars adorned selected pieces of furniture around the room. Rugs covered the wooden floors. A lace runner fringed the edge of a mantle above the fireplace and family photographs and local pottery adorned the shelf.

Andzia, Stasha's younger sister, strolled around looking for ideas. She was the next to be married and viewed everything with overly romantic notions.

"I shall have to have some of these." Then, "Mama, will you make me another table cover? And I must have one of those... Of course, I will have a baby quite soon, so that I can have family photographs like Stasha's."

"Oh, for goodness sake, Andzia. Let the icing set on the wedding cake first," said Bronka, smiling and teasing her.

Two complementary wood-carvings and one of Stasha's prized possessions, a piece of hand-cut Polish lead crystal, sat on shelves affixed to one wall, out of reach of little hands. These shelves had originally been put up to take Andrzej's books. He had always enjoyed reading. One of his most guarded possessions was an old Star Atlas. Since childhood, he had always had a fascination for the night sky and this had not diminished in adulthood. Late at night, often when he was very tired, he would relax by sitting and dipping into one of his books.

He also exchanged books with neighbours and newer ones would be purchased from one of the Jewish bookshops in Mir.

Andrzej's slightly scruffy tobacco box appeared to have pride of place on a table by another large armchair. Stasha had tried unsuccessfully to relocate it many times but it always found its way back, so she had given up, admitting defeat. Stasha, jokingly but apologetically, drew attention to the box. The women reaffirmed their fellowship with light-hearted rebukes of, "Just like a man," and "Oh, I know," and "Well, what can you do?" They each added their own contributions.

"I'll swear he stands behind the door wearing his muddy boots, just waiting for me to finish mopping the floor." The women laughed. Then they converged on the kitchen to help with the serving of the first round of refreshments; this would be followed by a seemingly unending stream of appetising dishes. The kitchen also served as a large family dining room. There was a wonderful smell of food cooking and the open range was crowded with bubbling pots and pans.

"Has your water supply frozen yet? We've had so many

problems with ours this winter," said Elena, their sister-in-law.

"It was minus fifteen last night and was frozen first thing. We had to carry water this morning from a neighbour's supply. We have an arrangement with them. They border on our property but they are on higher ground and don't have the same problem we do," said Stasha. "A natural stream is our only water supply, and we are just hoping that the weather doesn't deteriorate further. We are lucky, they are good friends and neighbours and we all help each other out where we can. We need the favour again in spring, when the big thaw arrives. Our water supply turns green and is unusable for a while."

Although the families were without indoor sanitation, piped gas or electricity, they considered their lives to be rich and bountiful in so many different ways. They discussed their blessings at length.

The men began to drift into the kitchen, looking for more of Bogdan's elixir. "I certainly would not like to live in the city," said Bogdan. "I think I would find it quite intolerable compared to a life on the land. I know work is hard but you are in control of your own life, your plans and your future. Anyway, I don't like anybody telling me what to do."

"Quite so!" "Neither do I." "Nor me," were the resounding responses from the menfolk. "We make our own decisions that directly affect our prosperity and reap the rewards of our labour. Work harder, move up in the world."

There was a particular aspect of life that probably made those growing up in this area feel very secure. Practically all of the Polish families were of the same social status. The children attended the same school and their parents met and socialised. No one was immensely rich and no one was desperately poor. No one wanted for anything, because everyone had as much as their neighbours.

This was not the case for everyone. There were people in a village not too far away that had lived in this area before the Polish families had arrived. Quite a few of these White Russian families had resided here for decades and they were far from prosperous. When the Polish settlers had arrived, many of the Russians were living in abject poverty. They had very little, and never enough to eat.

"I do feel sorry for some of the local Russians," said Stasha. "They don't even possess a pair of shoes between them. They walk barefoot in summer, and in winter they bind their feet with rags and string. It's the children that I feel for most."

Bogdan stood with his back to the roaring fire. "I would say that many of them are better off now that we are here. They work on our farms and we pay them well. Their situation was much worse before we came."

"Their farming skills were very poor, but then again they never had any aid or money to invest to improve things. We have been fortunate," said Andrzej.

At that time, Andrzej employed local Russians and paid them well, as did most of his fellow settlers. However, there were one or two farmers who had a reputation for ill-treating their farmhands and paid helpers. This did not go unnoticed and, in years to come, they would regret it.

The family enjoyed a lovely weekend. Chatting, singing, dancing, eating, drinking, a little bit of arguing and a good time was had by all. Andrzej had a good, strong voice and he and Stasha had sung to the children since they were born. Singing came very easily to the whole family. Practice, confidence of expression and a lack of inhibitions had virtually turned the family into a choir.

Being a large Catholic family, there was often a name day to celebrate. Instead of birthdays, the children would celebrate their Saint's Day. Today was St Benedykt's Day, so it was Benek's turn. They raised the roof with quite a few choruses of 'Sto lat', the Polish equivalent of 'Many Happy Returns', a song the family sang at birthdays and weddings. After a few choruses the children shouted "Again! Again!"

Sto lat, sto lat, niech żyje, żyje nam,
Sto lat, sto lat, niech żyje, żyje nam,
Jeszcze raz, jeszcze raz,
Niech żyje żyje nam, niech żyje nam.

(Good health, good cheer, may you live a hundred years, one hundred years.)

It was time for Stasha's family to leave. It had been a busy time but they had all enjoyed it very much, especially the children. Stasha announced that she was pregnant yet again and the baby would be born in spring. This would be their sixth child.

5. LIFE IN THE OSADA

To reap what you sow

They named their sixth child - a pretty, fair baby girl –
Leokadia, known as "Leonia". Stasha had her hands full now,
but the older children were good and Andrzej took on even
more labourers. Stasha had always helped with the milking
when able as it was performed manually and was very time-
consuming.

Andrzej was in the yard, fixing a gate when heard a
commotion in the milking stalls. He stopped what he was
doing and ran to see what was going on.

"Stasha! What happened? Are you all right?"

"I am totally fed up with that bad tempered animal. My
nerve is broken. She has donUntil e this once too often. I've
been kicked from one side of the stall to the other, I'm
covered in milk and I have had enough."

Andrzej picked her up and dusted her off. "No more
helping with the milking for you, others must do it. I am not
having you putting up with this any longer." He noticed for
the first time how tired she looked and realised how much
work Stasha did around the farm and how she rarely
complained. He must hire more help.

They settled back into their usual routine. One Saturday
morning, although the weather outside was good, Stasha

noticed that Jozef was following her around the house like a little shadow.

"Is everything all right?" she coaxed.

"Oh yes, Mama. Everything is well." The silent, close stalking continued.

"What is it, son? Come on, out with it."

Suddenly Jozef blurted: "Mama, can I have a dog?" Stasha was taken by surprise; they had so many animals to look after and feed as well as an ever-growing family.

"Oh Jozef, I'm not sure this is a good idea." As soon as she'd answered, she found she could not ignore his profound look of disappointment. As she looked at her first-born, she considered that he never asked for much and became uncomfortably aware that the constant new additions to the family meant ever-diminishing attention for him. She said, "I will ask Tata, let's see what he thinks."

The minute Jozef saw his father, he asked, "Has Mama asked you about my dog?"

"What dog, Jozef?"

So he explained to his father that he had seen a litter of pups belonging to a White Russian family living nearby.

"They are going to drown the puppies if no-one will buy them. I have saved my zlotys from doing my chores and I have enough to buy him. They want five zlotys, so may I have him, Tata?"

Andrzej discussed this with Stasha and they decided, albeit reluctantly, to allow Jozef to have the pup. They did not want to encourage a sentimental attitude towards animals but they knew that the children had to learn to respect and look after certain animals, as well as being taught that they must also slaughter others for food. Jozef was already used to watching his father kill a chicken because it had stopped laying and they all knew that the old broiler would go in the family stew pot for dinner.

As soon as he was told that he could have the dog, Jozef ran all the way to the tumbledown shack where the Russian family lived. He offered them three zlotys and they accepted four. He arrived home with the dog on a piece of rope. The family gathered around to greet and inspect the new puppy.

"I am going to call him Zuck (beetle) because he's shiny and black like a beetle," announced Jozef. The little Labrador soon became part of the family.

Another year came and went. The days grew warmer as summer was on its way. The children were all huddled around their father in the stable as one of their mares was about to give birth. This happened quickly and without any problems. However, Andrzej soon realised that this was because the foal was exceptionally small. As the children squealed with delight and took turns touching the tiny creature, he knew what he must do. Without a word, Andrzej got up and went into the house. When their father reappeared a few minutes later, he was carrying his shotgun. Mama was at his side.

Mama spoke. "You must say goodbye to the little foal. We cannot keep him."

Tata followed up with, "Say goodbye and then go into the house."

Panic set in. "Why?" "What for?" "No Tata! No!" "Mama, don't let Tata do it."

"It is better sooner than later. He will only suffer and you will get more attached to him," said their father.

"Please Tata, don't. Don't shoot the baby horse," were the unanimous cries from the children.

Then he explained that the foal was too small to reach its mother's milk and would starve and die.

Benek pleaded with his father, "Tata, don't shoot him. I can help to raise him. I can feed him with a bottle. Jozef has Zuck, I can have the foal. Please? Mamma, tell Tata that you will help me."

"I think Mama has more than enough to do, don't you, Benek?" said Tata in a stern voice.

Andrzej stood and looked at his brood. There was Mietek, whose face was always dirty whatever they did, and Cheshek with streaks of tears down his face and Leonia crying, with a runny nose. He tried hard to be firm and say no.

"I will help him, Andrzej," said Stasha.

"Oh, go on then. Welcome to the mad house." Andrzej walked away, looking at the sky, shaking his head, mimicking great disdain. This made the children laugh and their tears turned to joy as they jumped up and down on the spot.

For many weeks following this, every day Benek would feed the foal with a bottle until he grew and thrived. Benek named him Cashtan.

Life moved at a purposeful pace and an air of contentment settled on the Gwizdaks and the whole community.

Jozef and Janina were now aged ten and nine. It was time for their first communion. Andrzej and Stasha had decided that they should be confirmed together. This was the first communion of children from Puzieniewicze. New clothes and shoes were bought, so that the children would look their very best for the group photograph. Janina had a white confirmation dress complete with white headdress. Jozef wore a white shirt and dark trousers. Later on, they all looked so serious on the photograph holding their communion candles.

Everyone received gifts from their parents. Jozef's gift was a watch. It was not new, but his father said it was very precious. It had been broken for a long time but Andrzej had taken it into Mir and the Jewish watchmaker had repaired and restored it and replaced the strap.

"Look after it, Jozef. It belonged to a man who was the best friend a man could have." And Jozef noticed that his father looked sad.

All the family attended the Catholic Church in Mir, with the rest of their community, and it was a very proud day for everyone. A party was held afterwards and the children had the best of times.

A few weeks later Andrzej attended a military reunion with the men from his village, as he had done regularly over the years. They received notification saying that their hero, Marshal Jozef Pilsudski, was to visit the neighbouring province of Nowogrodek.

When the day arrived, without hesitation, the men from the Osada went to meet him on horseback. To the great surprise of the assembled dignitaries, they unharnessed his horses and hitched themselves up to his carriage and hauled him to the Town Hall amid much singing, shouting and celebrating. They had not forgotten how he had led them to victory and this, in turn, had resulted in better opportunities and a new life for them all.

After all the recent excitement, things settled back into a settled routine. It was a hot summer's day and Jozef and Janina were out in the fields picking vegetables and growing thirsty.

"Race you back to the house." Jozef made sure that Janina never won. She was taller than he, and since he was a year older than his sister, this bothered him. They dashed into the kitchen and started to search through cupboards. Jozef found a juice bottle and took a big gulp. Within a minute or two, he started choking. He fell to the floor, writhing and kicking. Janina was terrified. She ran out of the house to find Mama or Tata, shouting, "Help, please come, something has happened to Jozef."

Pandemonium broke out.

Jozef, the beekeeper, was passing and was alerted by the commotion. "What is it Andrzej? Is there anything I can do?"

"Get the doctor. Please hurry."

"What shall I say has happened?"

"Tell him Jozef has drunk something. Please be quick." Andrzej in his panic wondered if he should have sought out another neighbour but there was no time to spare. His mind was set at ease when he saw his neighbour running down the road, leaving a dust trail in his wake.

Stasha was beside herself and did not know what to do. Usually a very practical mother, having nursed her children through many ailments, in this instance all she could do was wait and watch as her oldest son lay on the bed where his father has carried him.

"What was in that bottle, Andrzej?" Stasha asked desperately.

"A concentrate for horse fever," said Andrzej, barely audible.

They had been unable to make him sick and when they tried to give him water he could not swallow anything. The doctor lived some distance away and by the time he arrived the poison had been digested and Jozef was unconscious.

"I do not know what the prognosis or the outcome will be. We can only wait. He has had a severe allergic reaction to the substance as well as the poisoning. I suggest that you send for the priest, as he may not last the night. There is nothing more I can do."

Stasha and Andrzej kept a vigil throughout the night as Jozef lay in their bed. Janina and Benek could not sleep and spent the night pacing and looking in on Jozef.

"Will he be all right, Mama?" asked Janina.

"We don't know, my love. Go back to bed," said Stasha. "And say a prayer for your brother."

The next days were the hardest they had encountered as a family. Stasha could not stop the tears from pouring down her face, which made the children weep afresh.

Andrzej was helpless, which made him angry. He hated a situation that he could not put right and his frustration boiled over.

"Can't you do something more useful, Stasha? That constant praying is driving me mad," yelled Andrzej at his stricken wife.

"You should not have left that bottle where the children could get it." As soon as the words had left her mouth, she wished she could take them back. "Andrzej, I didn't mean it, I just feel so helpless. I am sorry, I know it was an accident and no-one's fault." Stasha expected him to comfort her and say it was all right but he just stormed out of the house in silence.

After a few days, Jozef seemed to stabilise. His temperature had returned to normal and although not fully conscious, he was beginning to stir.

Then one morning, a loud cry brought his mother racing to his bedside. "Mama, Mama, I can't see. I can't see properly."

Jozef had regained consciousness but at the expense of his eyesight. The poison had left his vision severely impaired. Stasha tried to hide her panic from her frightened son.

No one knew whether or not his sight would improve.

Over the next few months, the family tried everything they could to help the situation. Zuck, Jozef's Labrador, seemed to know that there was something wrong and stayed by his side throughout. Once he was well enough to get up, the dog helped him to get around the house. When they went outside, he was always with him.

Andrzej and Stasha took Jozef to see as many doctors as they could find within a reasonable distance of their home but no one could help. They seemed unsure of what had happened to his eyesight and how it should be treated.

After a few months, he regained some of his vision but his eyesight was still very poor. Jozef had also lost months of schooling and this was starting to distress him further. He confronted his mother one morning.

"I will not be able to join my class and will be put down a year, as I am too far behind. I know it. That happened to Erik when he was ill for a long time. Mama, I can't go back to school as the other children will laugh at me. If I am held back, they will say I am a dunce."

Stasha would not give up. She visited one eye specialist after another. Finally, after a train journey to Vilnius, quite a distance away, they found a doctor who gave them hope.

Jozef had developed opacities clouding the corneas of his eyes. He was admitted to hospital and treatment was started straight away. Within a few weeks his sight started to improve. After a couple of months, Jozef's sight in his right eye was nearly back to normal but he had scarring on his left eye. The condition was permanent.

Jozef was soon back at school although he was not happy at being held back a year. Because of this he was teased and bullied by the Machniewski boy. They had been good friends when they were younger.

Stasha was in the kitchen, brushing the children's shoes for school the next day, when Andrzej came in. "I am worried about Jozef," she said. "He is so upset by this boy at school. I wonder if we should speak to his parents."

"I don't know, Stasha, this sort of thing has always happened. Perhaps it is just part of growing up and something that many of us must learn to handle. I am not sure that many parents take kindly to criticism aimed at their children. I don't know what good it will do."

Stasha remained worried, as Jozef was no longer the happy little boy he had once been. However, she was relieved that he was now well. This ordeal had been further complicated as the family now had another child, sibling number seven, Apolonia (Pola), a beautiful baby girl with a mass of dark hair.

Another summer came and went and Stasha gave birth to her eighth child, an adorable little girl named Regina (Gina). By this time, Stasha was growing weary of childbearing. It was dangerous and exhausting without the help of midwives or medical care, only the support of local women who assisted each other through labour and birth.

Luckily, she had never encountered any real problems but

still the toll on her body and the constant demands on her time and strength were enough. She found it hard to believe how she managed on so little sleep and got through so many chores in a day.

One can well imagine and understand the reluctance of a woman to respond to her husband's desire for affection after bearing eight children. As a good Catholic wife, however, there was little room for denial. Recently, it had become easier to use weariness as a reason to resist the possibility of yet another child. For the first time in their years together, their closeness was at risk.

A good wife and mother has to share her attention among everyone. The children are her first concern and there is never enough time left for a husband and wife to be the couple they were at first. A husband can easily come to feel neglected and cast his eye in another direction.

The beekeeper's wife was only kept busy when she was potting and selling honey. They did not have a large family. She spent much of her time curling her blond hair and preening herself. Her feckless husband neither noticed nor cared, so she was constantly on the lookout for someone to pay her attention. Whenever Andrzej called at the house for honey, it was noted that his horse and wagon stood outside for a considerable time.

Eventually this was brought to Stasha's attention. She was upset, distrustful and felt isolated. Stasha knew these feelings could be self-destructive if not sorted out but, then again, drawing attention to the matter might only invite more trouble when a possible flirtation might burn itself out.

She worried over this for quite some time in private sadness, considering confronting Andrzej with her suspicions. However, she knew that if he was attracted to the beekeeper's wife, he would feel guilty and resent Stasha for realising this.

Alternatively, if there was nothing in it and she was just feeling vulnerable, she would come across as a moaning wife and this could distance him from her. She decided to say nothing but still felt unsettled. She knew she must find more time for herself. Her youthful looks were slipping away but that was only more reason to make herself feel wanted.

She had so much to do but even so, she decided to involve herself more with others. She was part of the Mothers' Union and she made the decision to meet with them more often instead of sending her apologies.

"Andrzej, have you heard the news?" Antoni Swiercz, the local administrator and a close friend of the family, had called at the Gwizdak house.

"Hello Antoni, how are you and the family?"

"We are all fine, thank you. Sad news, I'm afraid. We have just received a call at the office. Marshall Pilsudski died yesterday". Both men stood for a few moments as old times, back in the field of war and life up to the present day, flashed through their minds like drowning men.

These strong, fiercely independent men, suddenly let their tough exteriors fall away and with outstretched arms, came together and hugged each other firmly.

The men from the village had gathered in the evening in the community hall. A spokesman echoed their thoughts: "How can we commemorate this great man?"

Antoni Swiercz spoke up: "I will contact head office and ask if anything is being planned.

The following week, the men met again. The outcome of this was that some soil would be collected from under the cross in the village and sent by post to Sowiniec near Krakow, where a 100 metre high Memorial Mound was to be built from soil collected from all over Poland.

Stasha volunteered to help out at the pre-school kindergarten that had recently been set-up in the new community hall. This was ideal for her, as she could take Gina along who was now nearly four years old. They were prosperous and more help must be hired to do the chores around the farm.

"Stasha, I am so glad you decided to join us at the nursery. We have always struggled with feeding the children. I don't know what some of them live on." Lidia Czyz, a neighbour and a good friend, was chatting with Stasha as they helped to prepare the children's lunches together. "You have a reputation for being an excellent cook and now I can say I know that to be true."

"I've always enjoyed cooking, especially with company and help. Having always been part of a large family, I find that meal times are the centre of family life. It's very important to me. It's the time when we sit down and talk to one another," said Stasha.

It was a warm sunny afternoon and one of the parents had brought along a camera. Stasha and the two other assistants posed for a photograph with the children outside the community hall.

As they walked back into the hall, Lidia said, "Now this will surprise you. Do you know what I heard yesterday? Zofia is pregnant. So the old beekeeper has got it in him after all!"

Stasha later looked at the photograph, wondering why she hadn't removed her apron. She smiled as she saw her youngest child, Gina, sitting in the middle of the front row with her shiny, dark hair.

Stasha, along with the other women, had helped to influence many of the changes in the community. As well as the nursery, they also had a village bakery. At one time each family had baked their own bread but now the Slowaski family supplied bread for the whole village.

What they could not acquire within their own village was available nearby. Turzec was a largely Jewish village just five kilometres away and they now had regular deliveries of anything from oil and coal to pots and pans. Travelling Jewish merchants were a regular sight in the area and they carried everything imaginable, or so it seemed to the children. However, the families had to travel to Mir, the nearest large town, to purchase items such as shoes, saddles, children's bikes, etc.

The Catholic Church was also in Mir but this was too far for them to visit on a regular basis. The community only travelled there for important religious services and festivals. The community hall in Puzieniewicze served for all locally held meetings and socials. It also housed the village library. At this time it was the only place that housed a battery-operated radio and the villagers gathered there regularly to listen to popular radio programmes, although the children thought that the radio was rubbish, because the adults chose the channels. There was a wind-up gramophone at everyone's disposal; the children enjoyed this more. Monthly dances were held and there was a great deal of musical talent within the community. Many men played the accordion or violin.

There was talk in the community about plans to build a swimming pool and sauna within the next couple of years. Things were really moving along.

6. CHRISTMAS 1937

Everyone was looking forward to Christmas. It was a Thursday in early December and Benek had stayed late at school as he was rehearsing to play King Herod in the Christmas pageant.

Benek stood on stage, straight and tall as he had been told, trying to look important and regal in his gold cardboard crown, when another teacher burst in. Benek saw him talking anxiously to his own teacher and then they both looked his way. The other teacher turned and left.

"Now I want you all to remain quiet for a moment. Benedykt, please come here, I need to speak to you," said Miss Radziewieczona, his teacher. "A neighbour is waiting. You must go home straight away."

"What has happened? Is it my mother?" asked Benek, who knew that his mother had been unwell for the last few days and had to lie down now and again.

"I cannot say more, you need to go home now."

Benek saw the neighbour in the hall. "What has happened?"

The neighbour just shrugged his shoulders and held out his hand.

Benek was now very worried and convinced that something had happened to his mother. The School was in the nearby village of Latki in a building that had been a Russian field hospital in the First World War. Benek did not walk back with the neighbour but broke free and ran the two kilometres home as fast as he could. He did not pick up his coat - and the cardboard crown was found later on the road outside the school.

Meanwhile, Jozef was at Uncle Bogdan's house near Mir. Uncle and nephew were very close. Bogdan often said that he was like the son he never had. Jozef was also very friendly with his cousin Klara and often stayed over with the family.

Jozef had just had a sip of the illicit vodka. Bogdan was showing Jozef where he kept his hidden still when Andrzej burst into the house.

"Jozef, get your things. You must come home straight away."

"What is it, Tata? What's happened?" asked Jozef.

His father would not answer. "Don't ask son, just do as I say."

"Anything I can do, Andrzej?" Bogdan saw that his brother-in-law was extremely agitated and distraught.

"Come over later, Bogdan, and bring Bronka with you. I'll see you then." Andrzej rushed out of the house with Jozef in tow.

Earlier that morning Leonia had been unwell and did not go to school. The day before she'd had a headache, so Mama said it was better to keep her at home so she would not miss out on the Christmas activities at school. As Stasha herself had not been feeling well, she thought that she and Leonia had a virus.

They arrived home and, before Andrzej could stop him, Jozef ran on ahead. He was immediately confronted with a large cross standing in the hallway. He turned to see the priest and his mother. Somehow, instinctively, he knew what had happened. He could not mistake the look on his mother's face.

"Leonia?" He said her name and his mother's head

dropped instantly. The doctor had been and could do nothing.

At that moment, Benek arrived, having run all the way from school, puffing and panting and hardly able to breathe. "Where is Mama? Is she all right?"

His father spoke. "Son, it is not mamma. It is Leonia."

"Mama, what has happened to Leonia?" asked Benek.

"God has taken her," said Stasha, through her tears and heartbreak.

There was silence for a moment.

"Then I shall never speak to God ever again!" shouted Benek.

And as time would tell, he never did.

The family was shattered and tormented by their loss. Their pretty Leonia, always smiling and skipping, had been a happy little girl. They recalled how she loved to pick peas and they would hear her singing in the garden. She had had the most beautiful singing voice. It was beyond belief that one of their own was gone, so suddenly.

It had been quick: was that a blessing? Leonia had not had a virus. The doctor said she had suffered a brain aneurysm. A blood vessel had burst and nothing could have saved her.

The family travelled to Mir and Leonia was buried in the graveyard of the Catholic Church. Stasha recalled that this was where all the children had been confirmed. She recalled how Jozef and Janina had been amongst the first children from Puzieniewicze to be confirmed. How proud she had felt then. How smart they had looked in their new clothes. Jozef was pulling a face in the photograph and Janina looked so much older than she was.

On this terrible day, she tried to reflect on how far they had come and remember all the good things that had happened but the black cloud would not lift and she felt her misery in the pit of her stomach: festering, painful and sore. She prayed to God for some relief.

Weeks passed and life continued in its usual routine. Jozef

was very concerned for his mother. She would wait at the window to look for Leonia to come home from school every day, until the silent tears would begin to flow down her cheeks. Her eyes were constantly swollen, she would wring her hands and nothing anyone could say was of comfort to her.

Then one day Jozef, who had felt the frustration building up inside himself, could no longer stop it from boiling over. He was so angry at his helplessness; there was nothing he could do to fix this, nothing he could do to help his mother.

"Mama, Leonia is dead, she is not coming back. You must stop watching for her to come home from school. She will never come home again."

A shocked silence ensued as mother and son stood and looked at each other. Then Jozef apologised and put his arms around his mother as her whole body shook with sobs.

"It is all right son, I understand." Stasha never again stood at the window.

Slowly, her smile returned and they knew she was getting back to something like her old self when she picked up the tea towel. When the children would not do as they were told, Stasha would rap them round their ears with it. Its knotted tassels caught painfully at their ears and they knew they had been punished.

Spring brought newness. The big thaw was over. There was no more green water. Ice had been collected from the river and stored deep underground with straw, ready for cheese storage throughout summer. Cheeses were matured in a deep, subterranean vault located underneath an outbuilding between neighbouring farms. Thousands of cheeses had been produced during the previous year. Cartloads were taken to market in Turzec and Mir and from there the surplus was exported to the United Kingdom in exchange for Remington typewriters, which had been designed to accommodate the requirements of the Polish alphabet.

Their surplus of pork had also been exported and the returns on this were excellent.

Andrzej owned a good share in the Cheese Co-Operative Society and had made a healthy profit over the last few years and, as a result, was now set to purchase the extra land. This would extend his estate to over forty-five hectares. He sat in his kitchen with a mug of steaming tea, checking his accounts.

Stasha entered the room. "Things are looking fairly good Stash. With eight children to support, we need to expand... " He stopped, suddenly remembering that there were now only seven. Life had a way of delivering little stabs even during happy moments.

Stasha and Andrzej looked at each other. He stood up and pulled her towards him, holding her head to his chest. "We will never forget our singing princess..."

He returned to his books, whistling the tune he used to sing to his young daughter who was no more, the song he had sung to all of his children when they were small.

7. AUTUMN 1938

Unsettled times

Another good year brought what promised to be a bumper harvest.

Jozef was now sixteen and had been recruited into the Police Force for his national service. He had his uniform and was deployed in searching for foreign aircraft flying over the area. At first this sounded like a great job but, before long, intelligence began to seep through that all was not well in Europe. Aircraft sightings began to increase and the atmosphere was threatening. Even so, like any young man, his mind was focused on the dance he was planning to go to on the following Saturday.

This was to be a big event. Even some of the local Russian residents had been invited. These locals were not usually included, only those whom the elders of Puzieniewicze considered to be of a higher social class, such as the head of the White Russian community.

"There will be some new girls at the dance on Saturday. Some of those Ruski girls are real good lookers." Jozef was talking with some of the other young police officers.

"All the girls I know are my sister's friends or girls I went to school with. They are all stupid and most of them are ugly," said Jan, a fellow young cadet.

"Well, so are you, Jan. So you've got no chance," said Eduard, another of their colleagues.

Saturday arrived. The only dampener was that everyone's parents were in attendance. Jozef hoped they would go home early. He joined his friends. Most of the older ones had been allowed to have a beer. Of course, they managed to sneak extra ones. When the music struck up, they were ready to take to the floor. They had already decided who they were going to ask to dance.

Jozef turned to Jan, "Look at her."

"Who? Which one?"

"Jan, I know you are stupid but are you blind as well?"

Jozef had been looking at the girl from across the room on and off for an hour now; more on than off. She had been looking back and smiling. She was beautiful, with wide, almond eyes, a full mouth and a mane of dark, silky curls tumbling down her back. She was simply dressed but this girl had no need for ribbons and bows.

"Would you like to dance?" asked Jozef, as if this was a State Reception in the Grand Ballroom.

"Tak," came the reply. She was a wonderful dancer. Jozef loved to dance; it made him feel even more alive. Her Polish was good and they chattered away.

Suddenly and quite alarmingly, a hand grabbed Jozef's shoulder and roughly pulled him away.

"What do you think you are you doing?" His father took his arm and dragged him away, leaving the girl abandoned in the middle of the floor.

Angrily, Jozef confronted his father. "Why did you do that?"

Andrzej led his son to a quiet corner. "Never ever let me see you dance with a Ruski girl again."

"What's all this about? Why, father? What has she done? What's so wrong?" asked Jozef.

"I will not discuss it. Don't ever question me on this subject again. She is not good enough for you," replied his father. "Look for someone from your own class, a nice Polish girl. I have not worked so hard for you to bring shame on us and throw it all away."

Until that day, Jozef had no idea that his father felt this way. Poland was such a multicultural mix of people. Borders had been moved so many times over hundreds of years that often people were left as a minority in what they felt had been their own country.

Jozef's own mother had been a part of one these families, born and raised in Lithuania, bilingual. The area in which they had resided had been under Russian control and Stasha had only been allowed a Russian education. Therefore she was not fully literate in Polish and was home-educated when the children were small. The family were aware of this. They all knew that Mama wrote Polish very slowly.

So, although it seemed that Andrzej treated all his fellow men and women equally, when it came to family he turned into the typical patriarch in dominating his brood.

Jozef felt annoyed and confused. He had heard his mother crying a few weeks before and there had been words about his father spending time with the beekeeper's wife.

Later that week, Jozef could not contain himself any longer. His outspoken nature had got him into trouble in the past but he still confronted his father. "How can you be so judgmental and tell me who I can dance with, when you are always spending time with that woman and making Mama cry? Give her up or leave us!"

Both father and son had to take a deep breath and walk in opposite directions. Nothing was said about the incident again. It was noted, however, that Andrzej never went to the beekeeper's house again and always sent one of the children to buy honey. However, there was always gossip in the village and certain feeble minded women would continue to say that Zofia's daughter looked like a Gwizdak.

A few weeks later, a different trouble was brewing; this time it was not to be a familial concern but national.

Everyone was talking about the threat from Germany and everyone hogged the radio and hoped that the situation would not worsen.

The rise of Hitler and the Nazi party, and troubles brewing in a very unsettled Germany, posed an imminent threat for all neighbouring countries. It was widely known that Hitler encouraged victimisation of minority ethnic groups, blaming them for Germany's problems.

In early 1939, it was known that the Soviet Union had tried to form an anti-German alliance with the United Kingdom, France, Poland and Romania but several difficulties arose, including the refusal of Poland, Romania and the Baltic States to allow Soviet troops into their territories as part of the collective security force.

With the failure of these negotiations, the Soviets reversed their policy and on 23rd August 1939, they signed the Molotov-Ribbentrop Pact with Nazi Germany. This took the allies by surprise. The two governments announced that the agreement was merely a non-aggression treaty but it was widely seen as a sign that the government of the Soviet Union could not be trusted.

Their vacillating choice of alliances said a lot for their integrity and reliability, or lack of it. Furthermore, a secret appendix to the Pact was to reveal that they had actually agreed to partition Poland between themselves and divide Eastern Europe into Soviet and German spheres of influence.

The Molotov-Ribbentrop Pact was a licence for war and a key factor in Hitler's decision to invade Poland. Hence, the unthinkable happened. On 1st September 1939, Hitler and the German Army invaded Poland.

The Polish nation had had only nineteen years of peace in a country they could call their home.

8. AUTUMN 1939

The nervousness of the community was tangible. The children could sense how distracted their parents were: edgy, a little short-tempered, everyone rushing around. There were many meetings in the community hall. Andrzej and his former army combatants now met as a potential defence force rather than an agricultural co-operative. This change of guise was sickening to them all.

They had built their "Nowa Zychie" (new life) with their bare hands. It had been backbreaking and heartbreaking at times, but it was theirs. The former brothers-in-arms were now husbands, fathers, friends, colleagues and neighbours. Was a settled life too much to ask?

Unknown to them, soon after the Germans invaded Poland, the Nazi leaders began urging the Soviets to play their agreed part and attack Poland from the east. The Soviets delayed for a number of reasons, the key being to allow Poland to weaken before making a move.

As Andrzej and his friends and neighbours huddled around the radio on 18th September 1939, they heard Molotov declare that all treaties between the Soviet Union and Poland were now void because the Polish government had abandoned its people and effectively ceased to exist. On the same day, the Red Army began to cross the border into

Poland.

The families of Puzieniewicze gathered together in the community hall.

"Where do we stand? I am most confused," said one of the village elders.

Antoni Swiercz, the village spokesperson, tried to console the group and reported the only information given to him: "The Soviets have not officially declared war on us. However, they now say that, as far as they are concerned, Poland no longer exists."

"That's rubbish."

"It doesn't make sense."

"I know."

Another landowner spoke up. "We have heard that the Polish government is now in exile. The Soviets say that since they have abandoned their homeland, it is left for the Russians to claim."

"What do we do now?"

"Would it be safer to welcome: the Ruskis over the Nazis?"

All these questions and more were flying around the room. The higher-ranking ex-army men still held a place of respect in the community and were considered in much of the decision-making.

The defence of their families was paramount and the men decided to join a united front and meet the Red Army before they arrived in the area, as a buffer. Word would be passed back, hopefully to ensure the safety of their women and children.

Village life and all its routines were thrown into disarray. There were some men left behind in the village, mainly the elderly, people who had settled in more recent years and a few of other nationalities. Nonetheless, order was breaking down.

Andrzej realised that Stasha would not be able to manage on her own. She could not run the farm and look after everything without his support. So, at the request of his parents, Jozef was released from his duties at the police station so that he could help his mother until his father's return.

Andrzej put on his old army uniform, picked up his rifle and his tobacco and left.

There was chaos in the local town of Turzec and news travelled back to the villages, causing more fear and trepidation. No one knew what was going to happen next. Stories began to circulate about Russian troops on the border mistreating people. Stasha was filled with dread: what was to happen to them?

Jozef came home. A semblance of order resumed, mainly to calm the children, although none went to school or nursery and mothers would not let their children out of their sight. Then word reached the village that their men had been arrested in a forest to the east. For a few days no more information filtered through.

Stasha and the other women would wait, worry and experience sleepless nights, a pattern that was to continue. The women got together and held their own meeting in the community rooms. They all felt a terrible sense of foreboding, but tried to remain positive.

"We all know that Russia hasn't declared war on Poland."

"Yes, we all agree, so theoretically our men cannot be prisoners."

"That's right. They are landowners and will be needed, now more than ever, to supply the area with meat, vegetables, cereals and dairy produce."

"True, especially now that there is a war."

"If we can continue as we are doing, do we all agree that feeding the Russian army is preferable to other possible outcomes?" No one wanted to announce their worst fears.

With a unanimous "Tak," the women hugged, prayed together and went back to their homes, feeling no more reassured.

A few days later, soldiers could be seen in the distance, approaching the outskirts of the village. As arranged, the families living on the edge of the village began to alert their neighbours in a chain reaction. If troops came, they had devised this warning system so they could gather up the children and join the nearest group. "Safety in numbers," they had all agreed.

"Who are they? Can you see?"

"What do they want?"

"Shout for the children, they're playing outside."

As the men neared their side of the village, Cheshek called out, "Mama, it's Tata. Tata is here!"

Mietek ran in doors to his mother: "Tata is home!" Andrzej had been spotted walking along the lane towards his home. Cheshek shouted again and the family ran to greet him. Jozef had killed a chicken the day before and was sitting on a stool with a bucket of hot water by his side, dipping the bird and stripping its feathers when he saw his father.

Andrzej entered his home with Stasha. The children followed. He was unwashed, cold, weary and silent. His uniform hung loose from his body. He stood in the middle of the family room, his arms wrapped around Stasha as if this would protect her and their family from the world outside.

Finally he spoke. "Stasha, I have to go and report to the police station in Turzec. I don't know how long I will be gone. I only have a little time. Russian soldiers are in the village and will come to collect us soon. Food has been short, there has not been much to eat where we have been held."

"Tata, I am hungry too," said Cheshek. Andrzej looked at his innocent youngest son and thought how glad he was that the child did not know the terror that he himself was feeling for them all.

"Then let's all have something to eat together, shall we?" The family sat at the table and had a hurried meal of bread, cheese and milk.

Stasha busied herself. "I'll pack some provisions for you

to take now. If you are not back by tonight, Jozef can bring cooked chicken and some more provisions to the police station tomorrow."

Andrzej turned to Jozef. "Hopefully we will get things sorted out and I will be able to return home. But if not, son, look after your mother and brothers and sisters."

"If not?" What did this "if not" mean? For the first time, the Gwizdak family was very frightened.

Janina brought her father all the tobacco left in his box.

Andrzej kissed the children and whispered to Stasha, who fought back tears.

"Don't go away again, Tata," said Gina, who at only four years old, was the baby of the family.

"I must, but just wait a while and I will be home again, you'll see." They said their goodbyes.

The following day, Jozef set out for Turzec. "I am going to ask at the Police Station on what charges they are being held and when they are to be released."

"Jozef be careful: don't cause any trouble." Stasha was quick to dissuade her eldest son from interfering too much. She knew all too well that he was headstrong and she feared for his safety.

"Mama, I am head of the family when Tata is not here. I will not stand by and do nothing."

Jozef went into town. The men were being held in cells at the Police headquarters. He spoke to a guard, who just barked at him in Russian. He soon discovered that the entire Polish Police Force in the area had been disbanded and arrested. Jozef realised with a shock that, had he not been granted leave to help to run the farm, he would have been taken away too and his family left to fend for themselves without any support.

He considered the most pressing matter was to try to negotiate the release of his father and the other men from the village. Jozef demanded to see an official. He was taken around the other side of the building and, to his surprise, was allowed to see his father through a window. They exchanged a few, brief words. Hurriedly, he gave his father the food parcel prepared by his mother and promised to return the following day with more supplies. Jozef resumed his enquiries with a guard who seemed to be in charge. He shouted orders to a couple of men who forcibly marched Jozef out of the police station yard and told him to leave the area and not return.

The following day he came back with tobacco and some more supplies. The building was empty. His father, along with all his compatriots, had gone.

Jozef left the Police Station and as he crossed the road he suddenly recognized someone. It was Katya, the Russian girl he had met at the dance. They stopped and looked at each other. She was still as beautiful as ever.

"I am so sorry, Katya", said Jozef.

She took his hand and said "So am I, Jozef.

"My father has been taken prisoner, I do not know what is happening. I am sorry that he acted as he did".

"It was nothing personal, I know that. I understand why he did what he did. He could not trust us and now this just proves he was right. Please take care, Jozef." And with that she turned and walked away. Jozef thought, please look back, just once. Before Katya turned the corner, she turned, smiled, waved and then her hand touched her lips. She was his first love. He would never see her again.

A few days later Stasha received a postcard from Andrzej. It had been posted in Stolpse about twenty kilometres from the village. It was obvious that the card had been censored; the words were stilted and sparing.

The entry of the Red Army into the eastern territories of the Polish Republic on 17th September 1939, and the Soviet-Germany treaty that divided Poland between those two countries, was to herald a chapter of unimaginable tragedy in the history of the Borderland Military Settlements and the entire Polish nation.

On the afternoon of that same day, 17th September 1939, leaflets (a grammatically poor translation of Russian to Polish) were dropped from a plane over the Puzieniewicze area, stating that "All landowners are to be crushed!"

News reached the village that Ukrainian and Byelorussian gangs were attacking many of the settlements, looting and killing. It was stated by the Russian Press on 20th September 1939 that, "The needy peasants are now settling their own grievances with their hated enemies, landowners, Polish officials and settlers." This propaganda only served to further inflame an already volatile atmosphere.

Russian peasants had always had difficult lives. They had never had the benefit of grants or support from their government. Their farming techniques were archaic and they were too poor to invest in anything that needed to allow time for a return. Theirs was a hand-to-mouth existence until the settlers arrived.

The Polish Government purchased the land allotted to the Polish military settlers in 1921 from Countess Umiastowska; it was not taken away from local people. In fact, the lot of the local people was improved by the possibility of employment on the settlers' farms and the chance to develop their own land with new farming techniques. Many had begun to grow their own vegetables and raise small amounts of livestock.

Prior to these events, relationships between the Polish settlers and White Russian community had been largely amicable and respectful.

It was widely perceived within the Polish communities at this time that warmongers had warped the truth to incite hatred and gain support for the Russian invasion.

Rumours and reports reached the area of atrocities committed in the towns and villages already plundered by insurgents. There were grave fears amongst the residents of the settlements.

They could hear the bombing of bridges over the River Niemen in the distance and the rumble of Russian tanks. Overhead, planes bearing the red star droned constantly.

Meanwhile, Russian officials, with support from the White Russian population, proceeded to carry out orders to strip all Polish settlers of their assets. Accounts in Mir Co-operative Bank, the settlers' banking facility, were frozen. All land, livestock, stock, machinery and supplies were to be divided up and distributed to Russian nationals already residing in the area and more moving in.

The army was now within days of reaching their settlement and the women decided to take their children and hide. They planned to lie low and see what happened when the army arrived.

Then news reached the area that one settlers' village had been attacked and all the residents had been killed, except a few who managed to flee to safety.

There was no time to lose: Stasha packed a few essentials and some supplies and the family set off to the house of an old friend. Zosia Grabowska was a widow who lived on her own. She would let them stay and if the army came across her house, which was quite remote, she did not possess much for them to take. Stasha had always helped her out in times of need and she knew that she could rely on her now.

Gina and Pola stood outside their house with Zuck on his lead. Stasha said, "I don't think it is a good idea to take Zuck. He may bark."

"Oh Mamma, please? We can't just leave him." The children were unsettled and frightened and Zuck did seem to be a calming influence, so Stasha relented.

The family trudged through the potato fields, the youngest ones, Gina and Pola, tugged along by Zuck. It had been a good idea to bring him after all. Pola stumbled and Zuck nudged her and pulled on his lead and guided them as the family walked in single file, making a track through the fields. The late crop was too high for the little ones to see over. Only Stasha and her older children could see the hordes advancing in the distance, as the Russian army moved towards their homes.

Janina had stuffed family photographs in her pockets. She had folded some of them and hoped they would not spoil. She feared the worse and did not know what would be left when they returned to their home. Most things could be replaced, but these photographs represented treasured memories.

They arrived at Mrs Grabowska's house. She saw them coming and came out to greet them. She was a kind lady and the children liked her. She smiled at them all, even though there was very little to smile about. She and Stasha hugged and held on to each other for a long time.

"Come inside, where it is warm. I have made a large pan of vegetable soup and lots of fresh bread. Come on, you must be hungry."

"Thank you so much, Zosia. It felt quite cold on the way here. We are all more than ready for this."

"Come on children, sit by the fire. Yes, it's much colder today. Then again, the first snows are only a week or two away," said Mrs Grabowska.

"Once it starts, we can say goodbye to clear roads until the end of March," said Stasha. "Our winters are so long."

"My old bones certainly feel it more these days," said Zosia. "Have you heard from Andrzej?"

"Only once," said Stasha, and then more quietly so that the younger children could not hear, "We don't even know where our men are."

The house was quite small and there was only room for Stasha, Gina and Pola to sleep inside. Jozef, Janina, Benek, Cheshek and Mietek would have to sleep in the barn. However, only a few hours after settling in for the night, they were all back, huddled in Mrs Grabowska's living room again. Pola and Gina were asleep, but no one else could manage to.

It had been too cold in the barn but even if it had been warm the strange and terrifying noises in the distance and their own fears kept them awake.

Stasha sat in the darkness. She cast her mind back twenty years, to the time just before she and Andrzej had met. Wasn't this just history repeating itself? Another war, but this time Poland was in the grip of defeat. The future was bleak and she forced herself to focus on the present.

She told herself that they would get through this a day at a time and as her lips moved silently in prayer, she closed by mouthing the names of her husband and all of her eight children and then made the sign of the cross.

Benek witnessed this out of the corner of his eye and felt puzzled. Was his mother asking God to keep everyone safe? Wouldn't mothers on all sides of the conflict be asking the same God to do that for them? Which side was this God on, anyway? It didn't make sense to him anymore.

The Russians had broken into the cheese store and there was not one of the 2,000 cheeses left. Anything that was worth even a trifling amount was gone.

The wooden cross, erected in 1928 in commemoration of Polish Independence, had been removed.

Cattle, horses, pigs, hens – in fact, all of the livestock – had gone. All the food stores had been looted. Homes had been broken into and many of the local Byelorussians had taken whatever they could lay their hands on. All that was left on the Gwizdak farm were two cows, probably because they were unable to move them, and an old mare named Cara. A stallion yearling of theirs was running wildly around the village.

Benek's Cashtan, the horse he had hand-reared as a young boy with the help of his mother, was gone.

When Stasha and her family arrived back at their home, it had been ransacked. Gina and Pola began to cry as they saw their mother's larder, usually stacked neatly with jars and sacks, now empty except for a trail of mess.

Flour and grain were spilt all over the floor, mingled with broken glass from jars, and piles and puddles of fruit and syrup. As they looked further, they found that there was no coffee or tea, nor was there any oil or coal. Even Zuck seemed wary and did not try to lick the food from the floor.

Jozef, Benek, Mietek and Cheshek immediately started to organise themselves in a bid to get firewood. Mietek came back from the barn carrying an axe; Cheshek followed with a smaller one he had found.

Stasha and the other womenfolk had predicted that this would happen. She had hidden some of their supplies in a store under the floor and most other families had done likewise. They would have to ration themselves, but for the present they were not in too desperate a situation. If their worst fear had been realised, and their house had been razed to the ground as in other areas, they would have been without warmth or shelter.

Stasha and Janina set about cleaning up and rearranging things as best they could. They would have to exist on subsistence rations from now on and scrape a living as best they could. The family had also hidden some money in their clothes and once the army had moved on and the threat from their Russian neighbours had died down, Stasha would try and buy a few essentials. Once this had gone, there was no knowing what they would do, as they could no longer draw on their substantial funds in the Mir Co-operative Bank.

There was a threatening atmosphere in the village and, although risky, Stasha and a few of her closest neighbours and friends arranged to meet up to discuss their problems and what they should do next. They discussed how they felt. Now they had to creep about, whispering in corners, as the Russian authorities were everywhere. The local Russian population was being encouraged to report on the activities of the Polish community.

"We saw Mr. Rosenberg passing through from Mir

yesterday. He said that a family down the road had told him that two soldiers had forced their way into their home, dragged their two daughters into the barn and brutally raped them. Their mother is beside herself and the girls are badly traumatised. They are so young."

The travelling Jewish traders, many of whom they could rely on and were long-term friends, like Mr. Rosenberg, had started passing through once more. Under the guise of selling household goods, they had already initiated a black market in other consumables, although there was not much money about. There was now a lot more swapping and second-hand dealing. One way or another, people were finding a way through. They looked for different ways to keep going and continued to help each other where possible.

Traders and relatives living in other villages brought news and stories from outlying areas. Terrible stories emerged of the fate of men from one osada.

Stasha and some of her closest neighbours were sitting in the back room of what had, until recently, been the village bakery, as their friend Danuta Slowaski related a story from her cousin.

"Their men had been rounded up and marched away."

"Then a dog found his owner's cap in a field and brought it to the man's wife. He led her to a mound of newly-dug earth."

She continued in a quiet, frightened voice. Shaking with emotion, she found it increasingly difficult to continue.

"He told me that the women in the village excavated the mound and found their men buried with terrible wounds. One of them was missing part of his face, and there were signs that some had been buried while still alive. They all had bare feet. With the help of a couple of local young men, the women wrapped the bodies of their men in white sheets and reburied them." She paused to control her voice. "Shortly afterwards, the two young men were led away and moments later, the women heard two shots."

The atmosphere in Puzieniewicze continued to be very threatening; within a few weeks a local man had been found shot dead.

One afternoon, shortly after this incident, Jozef and Benek were walking along a lane near a bordering farm. They were all eyes and ears, constantly checking their surroundings.

A gang of people appeared in the distance. Jozef and Benek knew to stay back and not to intervene. The brothers removed themselves from sight. From their hiding place behind shrubs, the brothers saw a gang carrying homemade clubs of heavy wood and what looked like tool handles. The brothers' first thoughts were to protect Mama and their brothers and sisters. They would be no use if they ended up injured or dead. This mob would take no prisoners, so the brothers stayed hidden from sight.

"What do you think they are after?" Benek whispered.

"Don't know," replied Jozef.

Suddenly, they saw a man near to them darting from one part of the field to another, trying to hide himself in a haystack.

"That's Mr Ziechinski. They've seen him."

"Joe, stay down. They'll see us."

"Yes, but I want to see what's going on. If they come near us, I don't want to be a sitting duck. I want to know so I can run like hell."

The brothers watched as the gang dragged their neighbour from a hayrick and stripped him to his underwear and began to beat him unrelentingly. In no time, the thugs were covered in blood. They could not see Mr Ziechinski as he was on the ground, surrounded. Eventually the group stopped, exhausted. Then one of them kicked him, threw down his weapon and walked away without a second look. The others followed suit.

Benek and Jozef waited until the perpetrators disappeared from sight and ran towards the battered man. When they reached him he was still alive but barely breathing.

"What should we do?"

"I don't know. They may come back."

They ran home and quickly discussed it with their near neighbours.

"What will happen if they come back and find that we have helped him?"

"Will the same happen to us?"

Stasha told her two oldest sons, "Perhaps you should go back and see how he is. We should not just leave him or we are as bad as his attackers. Take care, don't go near if you see anyone around."

When they reached Mr Ziechinski, he was already dead.

"Remember what happened to the two young men in that other village?" asked Benek.

"Yes, they helped to re-bury the men and then they were shot. We should get out of here as quickly as we can," said Jozef.

They covered Mr Ziechinski. In a hurry to get away, they did this as quickly as they could.

Later, when Stasha questioned them as to whether they had said a prayer for his soul, the boys told their mother that they had. They felt that their lie was excusable in this instance.

Mr Ziechinski, a non-military man, had employed the local White Russian people on his farm in the past. Everyone knew that he did not pay his workers well and had abused and mistreated them.

In the evening, when the younger ones were asleep, the brothers, Janina and their mother sat around the fire discussing the day's terrible events.

"I am so glad your father treated our workers with respect and paid them properly," said Stasha.

"Tata has always been a fair man," said Janina.

"We cannot rely on that any more. I trust no-one," said Jozef.

"Nor me," said Benek.

"We should be careful what we say to anyone now." With that comment Jozef made everyone aware that any security in their village was gone forever. "When people's backs are against the wall, only family count."

Stasha received another postcard from Andrzej. Thank God he was safe.

He said he had posted it near a railway station close to the Russian border. He could not say much, as before, but wrote that he was thinking of them and that he had run out of tobacco. The postcard gave her renewed hope. They would get through this and whatever happened, she would use her last breath to keep her family together.

They had started their married life with nothing but now they had the most precious thing in life to strive for: their children. They could start again under any circumstances as long as they had each other.

Christmas came and went. It was nothing like their usual celebrations, but more profound in a religious sense. The family prayed for Tata and for their own safety.

They asked to be reunited as a family and prayed in remembrance of Leonia. It was only their second Christmas without her. On Christmas Eve, they had shared "oplatek" (a religious wafer) and sung carols. Stasha and Janina gave the younger children little gifts that they had been able to make and barter from the travellers, and they managed to bake some of the special cakes and pastries they usually had.

"Snowflakes as big as bantam eggs have just covered six inches in the last half an hour," said Stasha. Then she finished her tea and retired to bed with the little ones, saying, "Goodnight and Happy Christmas."

"Goodnight, Mama. Happy Christmas!"

Winter was the coldest for many years. The snow was piled high around the village, where it would remain until March. The water was frozen and it was dangerous to stay outside for very long. A person could freeze to death in twenty minutes in one of these blasting, blinding snowstorms, aptly named "the whistler".

9. 10TH JANUARY 1940

You must leave

The families in the village had now spent the last few months waiting and worrying and trying to eke out their meagre supplies to last them through the long, hard winter. There had been no further word from their men.

"Mama, where do you think Tata is now?" Janina asked.

"I think your father and the other men are probably in Russia. The postcard came from a railway station near to the border," said Stasha.

"So, they won't be able to mail things from Russia because of the war, will they?"

"That's very likely. We do not hear from him because he probably cannot get a word to us now," said Stasha. "Try not to worry; your father will be alright."

Stasha was worried, but she was trying to stay positive. Their rations could not hold out much longer. Their future was uncertain. She tried, however, to retain a semblance of normality and calm. So, when Janina asked her mother if she could have a friend to stay, Stasha agreed.

Irena Krol was a very pretty girl. Jozef had carried her schoolbooks the previous year. Irena's family now lived in Zamosc, but the two girls had remained good friends and now regularly visited each other's homes.

Irena arrived and settled in and it was proving to be a good distraction from all the troubles. The family and their visitor were sitting together around the fire when they heard a commotion outside.

"What's that?" asked Stasha.

Jozef looked out of the window. "Russian soldiers. Loads of them."

"Can you tell what they want?" asked Stasha.

"I don't know, Mamma. It's chaos out there. I'll go and see what it's all about."

"Be careful, Jozef. Perhaps it's better not to interfere. We haven't done anything we need be worried about," said Stasha.

Janina looked over Jozef's shoulder. "They are stopping outside our house."

"They are coming up the path," said Jozef.

They heard hammering on the door.

"Keep calm. I'll go and see what they want," said Stasha.

"No, Mamma, let Jozef go," said Janina. "It might not be safe for a..." Janina managed to stop herself before saying any more. They had all heard too many stories.

The hammering continued. Jozef opened the door.

A soldier barked, "Gwizdak?"

"Yes?" Said Jozef.

"You have to leave. All of you. You have eight hours."

"Where are we going?" asked Stasha, who was standing behind Jozef.

The soldiers ignored Stasha's question and continued. "You have to get out of your house."

"But it's freezing. Where are we going in the middle of the night?" asked Stasha.

"Shut up. Just do what you are told and there will be no trouble. You can take 500 kilos of possessions per family. Wear warm clothes: you will need them where you are going. Take supplies to last for a month. Pack bedding, kitchen utensils and small agricultural implements."

Another soldier, holding a list, spoke. "You are to be taken to the same place as your men. Be ready to leave at four a.m. No personal items or possessions are allowed. They will be confiscated."

Jozef and his mother, now joined by Janina, stood in stunned silence. As they walked away, an older soldier looked back and said, "Leave your fancy things here. There will be no dancing where you are going."

"Oh my goodness," said Stasha. "It has come to this."

Irena, having heard all this, rushed up to Stasha in a panic. "Mrs Gwizdak, what will I do? How will I get home?"

Stasha, barely able to think straight, managed to say, "Don't worry, we will sort something out. I'm sure they will let you go home."

They all stood in the family room, looking at one another.

"We only have a few hours, we must get organised. We have a lot of things to pack," said Stasha, although she did not know where to begin.

"I'll go and get as many clean sacks as I can find," said Jozef.

"I'll help, Joe," said Benek.

"Yes, you do that, boys," said Stasha.

"Shall I get all the small tools together? Then you can decide what we need to take," suggested Mietek.

"Yes, that'll be good," said Jozef.

"Coming, Cheshek?" asked Mietek. His younger brother followed him out.

"You are good children," said Stasha.

Jozef spent the next thirty minutes dismantling a bicycle and putting it into a sack. Stasha and Janina frantically sorted out all their clothing, bedding and utensils. After a couple of hours, Stasha felt even more confused and disorganised than when she started.

"I cannot believe this is happening," said Stasha to Janina and Irena. "But at last we are to be reunited with your father."

"Maybe they will send us west. After all, the Russians

have already claimed most of this area."

Jozef had come in and heard this. "We cannot go west. The Germans have already taken that part of Poland. They will not want us in that area."

"Then I really don't know," said Stasha. She left the room to continue packing. She could get on better now the youngest girls, Pola and Regina, were asleep in the family room.

"Janina, what am I to do?" Irena was in tears. "How will I get home?"

"Write a letter," said Janina. "Whatever happens, we will get word to your mother somehow."

"Yes, then she will not be too worried," said Irena. "Anyway, I may still be able to get home on the day she is expecting me."

For a moment the girls were silent. Their minds were reeling. How many more people were leaving? Was it only the families whose fathers had been taken away? Were more towns being evacuated? Would Irena's family be sent away? Irena could not bear to consider any of this. "I'll write a letter now."

Janina went back to helping her mother. Irena was now occupied, which was good as she had already packed her small case containing her only possessions, and had nothing else to do but worry.

The hours raced by. There had not been time to check with many of the other villagers, but word had reached them and they now knew that they were not alone in being evacuated. Mrs Swiercz, the administrator's wife and her family were also frantically packing and many of their closest neighbours were doing the same.

Four a.m. arrived. Russian soldiers banged on their door with rifle butts, shouting, "Sobiraisya s veshchamy!" (Get ready with your possessions.) "You have twenty minutes, no more!"

The family had been hurriedly deciding what they should

take. Stasha and Janina organised small sacks of their remaining oats, cereals and other non-perishables. Even so, they only had enough provisions for a few days.

It was one of the coldest winters for many years and temperatures outside had plummeted to minus thirty degrees. The family was wearing as many layers of clothing as possible.

Then soldiers stormed their way in. "Out! Out! Leave your house immediately or you will be thrown out."

Pola and Gina were holding on to their mother's skirts, covering their faces. Mietek and Cheshek stood their ground in front of their mother, Janina and her friend Irena. Jozef and Benek put on a united front, as if shielding them all from the Russian soldiers. They understood the seriousness of the threats and the futility of resisting. As they ushered their mother and siblings protectively out of the house, the boys were roughly handled and brutally pushed out into the freezing night.

Horse-drawn sleighs were waiting with edgy-looking soldiers carrying bayoneted guns, herding everyone as quickly as possible.

Gina asked, "Mama, when will we be coming back to our house?" Stasha turned to her children. "We shall not be returning. They say this is Russian land now and we are a Polish family."

At the last minute, undetected by the troops, Jozef threw on the sleigh a sack containing the bicycle and another holding a horse collar that he had hidden some months back. He covered them with a blanket.

"Why are you bringing that, Jozef?" asked Mietek. "We don't have a horse." Jozef turned to him. "A horse collar is a good thing to barter with. Wherever we are going it could be more valuable than money."

One hundred and sixty women and children from their village, the wives and children of the arrested men, were told that they were being transported to Stolpse Station where they would be put on trains. At this point, none of the fearful and reluctant travellers knew what their destination or fate was to be.

Stasha attracted the attention of one of the soldiers. "My daughter's friend does not live here. She must go home to her own family. They will be worried about her."

"Too bad. Wrong place, wrong time. Get on with rest," shouted a Russian soldier with a heavy accent.

"But I can't leave my family. They won't know where I am," said Irena.

"Get on, now!" said the soldier as he raised his gun.

As they moved away from their house, Stasha turned to Irena and Janina, "We will try to get something sorted out at the station. Don't worry, Irena."

Irena, who at fourteen was the same age as Janina, gripped her friend's hand as her eyes filled, yet again.

"Mama, what is to become of us?" asked Janina. "Do you really think we will not be coming back?"

"We will start a new life somewhere else, with your father."

"It's not fair," said Janina.

"Our life has not been the same for the last few months, you know that. We can start a better life somewhere else. A place where we are welcome and where we belong. Somewhere where we can be a family again, all together with your father."

"Where will that be?" said Janina.

"I don't know. But better times will come," said Stasha. "We are leaving our life here behind now and moving on to something new. I came here sixteen years ago, a young married woman with a baby, your brother Jozef. Your father and I started with nothing, we have put so much into this place but I have no regrets. I am thankful to God for the many blessings we have had. We built a life here from nothing here and we can do it again. Good times will..."

Stasha's train of thought was interrupted and she stopped

speaking as she saw a group of local Russians waiting, ready to pounce and loot anything that had been left in their home.

At that moment, she knew that she would never see her home again. As the sleigh began to move more swiftly, she felt fearful but knew she must not show it.

Everyone was distracted by loud barking. "Look, Mama," shouted Gina and Pola, "Zuck's coming. He's keeping up." Zuck, Jozef's old Labrador, was struggling along behind. The snow was four feet deep in places and difficult to negotiate but he continued to follow them, running in the sleigh ruts. This made the young sisters giggle in their innocence, unaware of the seriousness of their situation.

As they approached the outskirts of the area, the vast scale of the exodus became apparent. Hundreds of people had been evacuated from villages and osadas all over the region. The snow had already been compounded by hundreds of tracks, resulting in a treacherous surface of packed ice.

They passed by a group of obviously traumatised people gathered around an elderly lady who had fallen and was unable to get up. Russian soldiers were urging and pushing them along, ordering them to leave the woman where she had fallen. Stasha knew what the soldiers were saying and was grateful that the children could not understand Russian.

She was sickened by the situation and her own helplessness but quickly assessed that there was nothing she could do. In their own dire situation, any action would be provocative and could risk the safety of the whole family. She had always been a person more than ready to help another in need but she knew that heroics would be foolhardy here. She felt terribly guilty and asked God to forgive her for her selfishness.

The group was being forced away from the elderly woman lying in the snow. "Move on! Go! We will shoot if you don't." Stasha saw the woman raise her head and look towards her family as they were dragged away from her. She reached out her hand as if to try to connect with them for one last time. Stasha saw a look of profound sorrow in her eyes as she disappeared from sight. Then suddenly, a single shot rang out. In an instant, absolute fear gripped them all.

Eventually, cold, wet and hungry, they arrived at the station. There were hundreds upon hundreds of people in a situation of utter chaos: people pushing, children crying as they were separated from their mothers, mothers screaming their children's names. The noise was incredible.

Bang! Bang! More shots rang out and silence fell. The Russian troops were now forcing people into waiting cattle trucks. Stasha saw that there was no escape. Seeing the look on her sons' faces she said, "Get in now, and help the girls. We need to stay together. If you hesitate, we may be separated. I need you to do as I ask."

Stasha took Irena's arm and approached a soldier who looked as if he was in command. "Excuse me, this girl..."

"Get on now, all of you. Now!" The soldier held his rifle lengthways to push them nearer the trucks.

Feeling ashamed at their weakness and inability to do anything about their situation, Jozef, Benek and Mietek could only help their mother and Pola, while Cheshek tried to lift Gina into the cattle wagon. Janina and Irena, feeling numb, climbed up without another word. They found a space and sat the youngest children down, then loaded their belongings. At that moment, Zuck jumped in next to them. This made Pola and Gina smile as they snuggled him between them.

"Come on Zuck. Sit!" said Gina as she stroked his head.

"Mama, Zuck's very wet. What can I dry him with?" asked Pola. Mamma, too preoccupied, did not hear.

"You've never been on a train before, have you Zuck?" said Pola.

A soldier appeared at the door. He had seen Zuck. "No animals allowed!" he shouted. This time, everyone heard.

"But this is Zuck, our dog," said Pola.

For a brief moment, the family looked at the soldier, then

at Zuck and then back to the soldier.

"Did you hear what I said? No animals." When no one moved he climbed onto the train and grabbed Zuck by the collar.

Zuck would not move his feet and started to make a strange mewing noise. The soldier jumped down from the truck and dragged the dog with him. The family looked on nervously.

Zuck struggled free and jumped back onto the train. The soldier was furious. He grabbed at Zuck and dragged him down once more. The soldier was still holding his collar as he struggled, yelped and tried to break free.

Then the soldier quickly drew his pistol and held it at Zuck's head. The children gasped and held their breath. A shot rang out and Zuck was instantly still. The soldier let Zuck fall onto the platform. Then he holstered his pistol and walked away.

Zuck was lying dead, in an ever-expanding pool of blood. There was an eerie silence for a moment as the family absorbed the shock. As they looked on, a small child's boot left a trail of bloody footprints in the snow. The crowd surged past, trying to avoid the carnage.

Zuck, their Zuck, part of their family - gone. The little ones had never known life without him. Now the horror of their situation had begun to dawn on them. One by one, the children succumbed to choking sobs. Jozef was sickened and could hardly control his feelings but he also knew that he must now act as head of the family and remain strong. His father had said, "Look after your mother and your brothers and sisters." He struggled for the right words.

When he spoke, it was in a controlled voice. "Zuck has gone and it was quick. If he had stayed behind, he would have starved to death. He would have been afraid and lonely before he died a slow and painful death. He is gone now and he will not suffer."

Then Mama said a prayer and everyone already in the

truck joined her.

Jozef felt the bitterness and anger well up inside him at the loss of the pup that he had wanted so much, bought with the four zlotys he had saved as a young boy. The dog that, at times, seemed like his only friend during the year when he had been almost blind. Bastards! Jozef's silent rage simmered.

His mother and siblings had read his expression. No one would dare to mention Zuck's name again.

The area was in a state of pandemonium. Thousands of bodies pushing and shoving, people falling and others falling over them. People losing bundles and packages, quilts and blankets, families losing children and being split into separate trucks.

The Gwizdak family had stayed put from the moment they had arrived and had not moved from the truck, the first one they had come across. They must have appeared to be anxious to go but they were astute enough to know that they had no choice and nothing to benefit from waiting in the cold.

Stasha was grateful that they were all together and she thanked God for this and asked him to let them join Andrzej wherever he was, as a complete family once again.

The children were still numb following Zuck's death. More strangers began fill their compartment; sixty people were crammed into an area hardly big enough for half that number.

People were being loaded like the livestock these transports were designed to house. Their new living quarters were dank and smelly and bore a familiar patina. Large, dried stains were recognisable from the cowshed floor back home. Animal and human excrement had stained these floors.

They saw some faces they knew. Another family from their village was being pushed into their truck. Stasha was friendly with their mother and the children had gone to school together. This brought a glimmer of comfort and normality to their situation. In the days to come they would be able to share stories from the home and the life they had left behind.

The large, wooden doors were rolled shut with the resounding crash of wood on metal and a large sleeper-like bar was levered across the outside to imprison the truck's fatigued and frightened occupants. They were locked in a pitch-black wooden box.

Eventually, after many hours of waiting and wondering, there was a screech of metal and the wheels slowly began to turn. The train soon picked up momentum and as they began to move faster, the wagon grew even colder. As it picked up speed, the extreme cold on the outside crept through the cracks in the wooden boards. Soon, many occupants found that their hair had frozen to the sides of the truck. There was nothing they could do, as there was only room for the children to lie down. The adults had to sleep sitting up. They rolled through the night and into the next day.

There were a few slatted shelves attached to the sides of the boxcar, forming makeshift communal bunks but nowhere near enough room for all the occupants. A small stove stood in the centre of the truck but there was only a paltry amount of wood to burn and they did not know how long it had to last, so they were frugal with the supply. In any case, the stove's heat seemed to dissipate instantly in the draught. A bucket had been placed over a hole in one corner and this was the toilet for sixty people.

Stasha woke after a brief sleep, drifting in and out of consciousness, checking the children and then falling back into nightmarish dreams. At the first moment of waking she was unsure where she was. Time stood still; there was no way of marking it here. For the first time in her life, she had no routine. Every day, on waking, there had been things to do right away. Now there was nothing. It was still dark. Her grandmother's watch, which had been given to Stasha on her passing, had been exchanged months ago for essentials, along with many more of their belongings. Now they did not possess a timepiece between them.

Stasha had exchanged her watch first, as Jozef seemed the least reluctant to let his go. It was only an old watch and Jozef had even refused a new one on his thirteenth Saint's Day. Instead he preferred to keep the old one his father ha\d given him. Stasha could not remember where this old watch had come from anyway. Andrzej had never said.

As she sat and took in the surreal scene, thin shafts of light beamed through splits in the wooden panels and over the huddled people as day began to break. The rays gave false hope of warmth to come. To Stasha, the light looked like something from a picture in a child's prayer book, conjuring up an image of an old man with a white, curly beard and flowing robes, reaching his hand towards a shaft of light that pointed the way to heaven. "And God spoke to Moses..."

Her mind refocused sharply on the present, to the box of people and reality, where the shafts of light only carried motes of dusty floating particles, the spirit and remnants of old souls gone before, now stirred up by its current cargo.

"Find something to do, Stasha," she told herself. "You've never had the time to daydream, but then again you have never had the time to dwell on heartbreak either."

As soon as everyone began to stir and waken, Stasha and the other women busied themselves with a task of prime importance: how to make the toilet arrangements a little more discreet and private. A debate ensued as to how this could be done.

"How can we attach a blanket to act as a curtain?"

"Have we anything that we could use?"

The problem was soon remedied with a penknife, a kitchen knife and a boot heel. It was also decided that it was better, for most of the time that the bucket should not be used. Only when they were in a siding, as they were at present, should they reinstate it. The rest of the time, the hole in the floor would have to suffice. In no time at all the matter had been resolved.

It was decided that it would be better if more of the women were seated near the toilet area as the young men and women in the truck would be less embarrassed to use it if the persons in the immediate vicinity were mothers or grandmothers. So the young people were encouraged to gather together in the daytime at the far end of the truck, away from the convenience.

Janina watched as the women discussed their problems and made decisions. She reflected that they were all part of communities that had built villages themselves from a patch of earth. Their houses were transformed into comfortable homes by the art of their own hands and the resourcefulness of their minds. Very few things had been bought as a completed item and improvisation was second nature to them all. They had grown together, as wives and mothers, into a community, helping and learning from one another. They could all help a child into the world and they all knew how to prepare someone to leave it.

Self-sufficiency had brought out the best in them. If they were only quite good at one thing, they would excel in another. It was important for one's standing in such a community to identify and develop personal attributes and skills that could be recognised, acknowledged and appreciated by family, friends and neighbours.

Janina knew that her Mama was respected not only for her many capabilities but also for her honest and caring disposition. Mama lived strictly by her own code of conduct, and by that of her Catholic beliefs. She disciplined her children, not sparing the naughty child who felt her wrath by way of the fringes of the tea-towel, but she was also very loving.

Although she was a God-fearing woman, Janina knew her mother would fight like a lioness if anyone threatened the life of one of her brood. At that moment in time, Janina realised just how much she loved her mother. A mother to which, as with many young women, she had not always shown respect.

She now felt very guilty and vowed to try and make up for this.

Her father, likewise, possessed the practical skills to fix, mend or create something out of almost anything. All of the men possessed a sharp knife and it seemed like a prerequisite of joining manhood that a boy would learn to carve basic items from a piece of wood. The Gwizdak children had watched as Tata had carved wooden skis for all the family.

Mietek had been able to swing a small axe and hammer a nail since he was about five years old. At times, Janina had witnessed Mama holding her breath as, being the most garrulous member of the family, he would be distracted while swinging and she was sure that one day he would lose a finger.

Tata would remind Mietek about his old friend, whom he lost a long time ago, who lost the top of his finger whilst chopping wood. This did not deter Mietek and make him more careful, he only wanted to know if the piece of finger was burned on the fire along with the wood.

Janina's brief interlude of distraction, pondering over her past happy family life, had helped to warm her heart. Now as the convoy rattled on, travelling further north, the temperature was dropping even further and she was brought back down to earth. The dreams and expectations of a fourteen-year-old girl did not include anything analogous to her current situation. Furthermore, thinking of her father had left her feeling insecure. Hadn't he always been there for them all, to sort out any problems they had? Didn't he always have the answers?

"Where are you now, Tata? I don't know what's going to happen to us and I feel frightened."

"Look Irena, I managed to hide some of our family photographs in my clothes. I have had to fold this large one of Mamma and Tata with Uncle Frank. I hope they don't spoil."

"I wish I had a photograph of my family. I don't know

when I will see them again," said Irena.

Janina had not meant to upset Irena. What a thoughtless thing to do. She had only meant to while a few minutes away.

They passed through Negoreloye and Minsk. At one point, the train stopped and a sound could be heard that was at first barely audible. It started to grow in volume: one by one the trucks were taking up the refrain of a traditional Polish song. This was when they realised that the convoy had just left their beloved Poland and was now on alien Russian soil.

Stasha and the children joined in. As soon as the song ended, the euphoria quickly faded and they were left feeling even more bereft. The higher their morale had been lifted, the further it had to fall.

Their future was now out of their hands.

The terrible sad truth of the matter was that, unknown to "Stasha" at this time; she would never see Poland again.

"Mama, I am cold." Gina, although the youngest, was usually the last to complain.

"Huddle in closer with Pola and me, and I will tell you a story." Stasha began to tell a story they had heard many times before. They listened intently, as children do, as if the ending was going to be different this time around. Mietek was eleven years old now and often attached himself to his older brothers in trying to be as grown up as they. Stasha saw his new vulnerability, as he joined his younger siblings and sidled up to his Mama and his younger brother and two sisters.

Through her maternal eyes, she still saw the baby he had been. Her son, the chatterbox, who could sometimes be so wilful. She felt great compassion as she looked into his face, now so very dirty. She kissed his head and pressed his cheek to her own.

After days of stopping and starting, they finally arrived at a station. They had no idea where they were. After a few hours, the toilet bucket was full and when the doors were opened they were allowed to empty the bucket, amid mocking and jeering from Russian troops.

Janina was indignant.

"What's wrong with them?" said Irena.

"They seem to think that normal bodily functions are unnatural and disgusting just because a person is a prisoner," said Janina.

"Perhaps they don't go to the toilet," said Irena, sarcastically.

"No they can't," said Jozef, who had been listening. "They are just arseholes anyway, so they don't need another one in their backsides."

Janina and Irena laughed, a rare sound in their current predicament. This seemed to attract unwelcome attention from the soldiers, who looked annoyed.

"Janina, be careful. Don't make anyone angry," whispered her mother.

Janina continued to whisper to Irena. "Yes, it is revolting having to use a bucket, but who forced that on us?" She continued in mock seriousness, "Will you join me, my dear friend, in praying to God that an epidemic of chronic dysentery strikes all the soldiers on this platform?" The girls collapsed in laughter once more.

Jozef looked across at the girls and then nodded his head towards the platform. "Arseholes, all of them."

The train rumbled on, deeper and deeper into the foreign wilderness. Utter misery was now slowly giving way to a little hope and some of the group was now adopting a slightly more positive air, perhaps borne out of an instinct to preserve themselves or their sanity, at least. One or two of the grandparents present were attempting to be a little more cheery for the sake of the children.

"Perhaps it will not be long before we arrive at our destination," said an elderly gentleman. "They say we are to be reunited with your fathers."

Their food rations had been used up and apart from some

millet a few days ago they had received very little. So they were optimistic when the doors were rolled back and they saw large, steaming pots brought onto the platform.

"Benek! Give me a hand and we will carry it back for the others. It's too cold for everyone to get out."

Jozef turned to the others around him. "Benek and I will collect your rations. Stay here and keep what body heat you have." Jozef and Benek were the first ones at the doors as they were unbolted and rolled back. They jumped down onto the platform. It was bitterly cold.

As Jozef climbed back onto the truck, with a bucket of soup in one hand, he grabbed an iron handle on its side to pull himself up. He cried out loud as his hand bonded to the freezing metal. In an instinctive reaction, he jumped back, tearing the skin from his palm where it remained glued to the handle.

In shock, he did not realise what had happened. Then a couple of minutes later, the blood began to flow and a sharp stinging set in. Miraculously, he was still holding the bucket of soup in the other hand. Mietek took hold of the bucket as Benek pulled Jozef into the truck.

"Jozef, let me look at that hand." Stasha immediately busied herself with the injury. "It wasn't clean to start with."

Janina added, "And goodness knows what else lives in this filthy truck."

They used a little of the greasy boiled water to wash Jozef's torn hand. That was all it was fit for. But the soup, and a lump of dark, hard bread was their only meal for the next two days. Although the oily soup repulsed Stasha, she knew that the children especially needed all the sustenance they could get, so she used a little salt that she had brought with her to flavour the gruel and soak the hard bread. The children nibbled it in little pieces. At least it would make the children thirsty and they would then, in turn, drink clean melted snow and this would keep them going.

"Mama, this is not nice food like you make for us at

home. I don't like it." Pola looked at her mother through the typical eyes of a six-year-old, as if to say, what else is on the menu, Mama, can we have something else?

"There is nothing else, Pola. Try to eat a little. It is better than going hungry." At least with something in their stomachs, they would have restful sleep. Well, as restful as they could in such cold.

Jozef said nothing about his hand but allowed his mother and Janina to inspect it and dress it with clean rags, torn from some of the bedding they had brought. Wounds heal better in dry climates and do not respond well to very hot or extremely cold conditions. Their damp prison and their lack of nutrition was not conducive to quick healing. The hand was to fester for a considerable time.

During the many days of sitting and waiting, the old men, women and children had nothing to do but to think, worry and wonder. They reflected on the lives they had left behind. This was a small comfort to them.

"Jozef? What is going to happen to us all?" Janina was looking more despondent than usual.

"Who knows? What I do know is that they wouldn't bother taking us all this way if they meant to get rid of us. They would have done it in Poland. So don't worry, my Jani." Jozef was outwardly consoling but he also knew there were fates worse than death.

A pattern was now emerging. The trucks were stationary for most of the day and travelled only through the night. They were barred from the outside. Although the prisoners could rarely see exactly what was happening, they could piece together parts of their journey from the sounds and the smells.

Jozef, Benek, Mietek and Cheshek were plotting what they might be able to risk doing and how far they would dare to push things at the next stop the train would make. There had been quite a few spasmodic stops by this point. Sometimes the train would sit in sidings for what seemed like forever. They knew that this waiting meant that Russian troop trains were being given priority on the tracks.

Their scheming was interrupted when one of the brothers needed to relieve himself. While they would all urinate in the bucket, or through the hole in the floor, not one of the three older boys would use this facility for a bowel movement. Two brothers would act as a screen, while the one indisposed would use his handkerchief and throw the soil out of a small hatch in the top of the truck. The smelly handkerchief was then stashed away and retrieved when needed. There was no water for hand washing.

However, their bodies had quickly adjusted to their poor rations. They were constipated and did not have to go through the humiliating routine as often as usual. When they did, their stools were small, dry and hard and they were thankful for that, as even this situation could have been worse.

The women had their own particular hygiene considerations to worry about and they tore the hems from their underslips to accommodate their needs.

After about a week into their journey, they all felt the oppression of stale air and body-odour. More than anything, they wanted to bathe. They could not clean their teeth or wash their hair and they were living and sleeping in the same clothes every day. Their baggage allowance had not allowed them many spares of anything and any clean items of clothing would now have to wait until they could wash their bodies

Mothers were huddled with their young children in a group near the toilet, when a woman spoke out.

"My mother is seriously ill. She has heart disease and all her medication is gone. She is dangerously cold and complains of bad chest pains."

"We can try to stoke up the stove," said one.

"We can warm a blanket on the stove and then wrap her in it," said another.

Knowing that this would starve the others of what little bit of heat there was, she said, "I cannot thank you enough. You are all very kind."

The older boys lifted the old lady nearer to the stove. The women managed to make her more comfortable and she fell asleep. After a few hours, she awoke and began gasping loudly, fighting for air. Her head went back as she struggled and her body convulsed, wracked with pain. Her family could only look on, helpless, as her daughter held her hand. Then with one last spasm, she collapsed, lifeless.

It seemed sad and disrespectful that she could not be laid out properly. The poor old lady's body lay in her own excrement and urine until they reached their next stop. Her corpse was unceremoniously laid at the side of the track. The trucks moved on once more.

Just over two weeks into their journey, the conditions were becoming intolerable. Their cold and hunger were at the limit of endurance. The train hurtled along, taking them ever deeper into Russia and further away from their home. They would now have to take more chances and risk all or they would not survive the cold much longer. Many people were very ill. More people began to die. An ever-increasing number of bodies was unloaded every time the train stopped.

Somewhere near Smolensk in Russia the train stopped and the doors were opened. After a brief spell to let icy, clean air in, the door was closed, but this time left ajar. Jozef, Benek, Mietek and Cheshek climbed down from the train and took a quick look around. There were no armed soldiers in their immediate vicinity. There were fewer armed guards at the stations now, as there was nowhere to escape to.

Cheshek spotted a small pile of coal. This was just the chance they had been looking for but Stasha would not let him follow his brothers, so he stood on the platform just below the truck door.

Jozef, Benek and Mietek formed a chain to pass the coal to Cheshek, who threw it into the truck. The brothers felt exhilarated. It felt so good to move around, to lift and carry and stretch their limbs.

Everyone had been confined to such a small space, unable to stretch or walk about. Although it may have conserved energy, there was a serious threat to their circulation and of muscle wastage.

One or two of the elders on the train were shouting to the boys, "Enough, enough. If soldiers come we can hide this. Anymore and we could be in serious trouble." However, just then, the decision was made for them. They heard the familiar screech of metal as the train started to move.

Jozef and Benek ran to get on. Mietek stumbled and fell. "Benek, stop! Mietek has fallen!" Jozef called to Benek who was just in front on him. They both looked at the moving train and back at Mietek. Could they make it?

The brothers did not give it a second thought. They ran back and grabbed their younger brother and dragged him up.

"I'm okay. Hurry", said Mietek.

Janina had pulled Cheshek back up into the truck. The brothers quickly jumped on themselves, as the train gained momentum.

"Shit, that was close," said Jozef. The train whistled along speedily as the brothers hauled the wooden doors to shut out the biting cold and the swirling snow. They looked down at Cheshek who was still lying on the floor. It was obvious that he was in pain. Then they saw the blood seeping through the tear in the knee of his trousers.

As he was pulled back onto the truck, he had caught his knee on a sharp metal hinge protruding from the side of the door. His knee was torn open and the wound was deep. Stasha busied herself tending to her son's knee.

The family glanced at each other, as they silently shared their thoughts: it was just one disaster after another.

As with Jozef's hand, Cheshek's wound was cleaned immediately. Some of the coal was put in the stove and melted snow was boiled.

"Sorry about your knee, lad. High price for a bit of bloody coal," came the response from an elderly man. However, the poor man paid a higher price during that same night. Even with the extra coal, as the fire died in the early hours, so did the old man. His body kept them company for a few more days, until they stopped and the doors were opened.

Stasha knew that the problem with Cheshek's knee was worse than Jozef's hand as the wound should probably have been stitched. As the days went by, Cheshek's knee became infected and he had difficulty standing.

10. MOSCOW TO SIBERIA

By the time the convoy reached Moscow, many people were weak and ill and beginning to succumb to hypothermia. Although this was horrific, it was a blessing compared to the suffering of many more who would, over the next few weeks, die as a result of frostbite and eventual gangrene.

One young mother, who'd had difficulty breast-feeding her baby daughter, had to sit and watch as the tiny infant died of starvation. She got off the train at its next stop, carrying her precious, stiff, little bundle. She took a few stumbling steps as the young woman accompanying her took over and tried to dig a hole in the snow with her bare hands. The ground was too frozen for her to make any impression at all, not even a shallow grave.

A Russian family, living unreasonably close to the track, were standing outside their dilapidated shack, watching. The local man started moving cautiously and slowly towards the mother of the dead infant. He held up his hand as if to say, "I mean no harm."

The Russian man, wizened and practically toothless, was followed closely by what may have been his wife and her mother. He had brought his shovel and began to chip a small hole in the snow. A look of profound sadness and understanding passed between the two families. It was obvious that the local family were desperately poor, as were most of the Russian people they had glimpsed from the train. In a silent but eloquent gesture of kindness, the older lady, the Russian babushka, held out an arthritic hand and offered two small, shrivelled potatoes to the grieving mother and pointed to her remaining child.

People from other carriages began to lift larger bundles from the train and place them on the snow. Stasha and Janina watched and prayed from the open door. This time, Stasha gave in to her feelings and allowed herself to express her pain through her tears. Stasha, Janina and Irena cried and hugged and wondered what the world had come to. Mietek, Pola and Gina, the youngest of her three children, were not alarmed at Mama's tears; they understood her compassion for others and took comfort in this.

There would be no crosses to mark these graves, no candles lit in memory. Only bodies abandoned in a frozen, foreign wasteland, lining the route of forced exile. Come springtime and the winter thaw, the sight would be horrendous and pitiful.

Stasha remembered Leonia, as she did every day. She was thankful that she had a Christian burial and lay in peace in Mir. She had been thinking of the many miles that distanced her from her dear daughter's grave. At first, she had felt that leaving Poland meant abandoning Leonia in her resting place. Now she knew that there was always someone whose suffering was worse. "Yes, Lord, I have a lot to be thankful for." Stasha spoke out loud.

Benek heard his mother and marvelled at how someone could be so faithful. He could not understand how she could be so thankful to a God who allowed all of this to happen, a God he had lost a long time ago.

The train ground to a halt at Vologda Station. From here, the line continued to Archangel, near the Arctic Circle. At minus thirty-five degrees, a body was past shivering and the cold was simply painful. The dishevelled group were aware that as long as they felt the pain, they would live. They knew that if the cold stopped hurting, they would die.

Guards ordered then off the train. This time there was no need for heavily armed soldiers as there was nowhere to run. The doors on the train had not been bolted for many days.

They would all stay together for the faint hope of shelter and food. Nearly half of the prisoners had perished during the journey. The surviving evacuees disembarked, many of them having difficulty walking. There were only enough sleighs to carry the weak and the children, although the poor horses drawing them looked close to death as well. Irena was forced to join the next sleigh after assurances that they would all be going to the same place.

At such a low temperature, walking can be an advantage and Jozef and Benek walked at the side of the sleigh for as long as their bodies would allow. Then they would hang on as best they could. Cheshek's knee was still bad and he rode alongside Mama with Mietek, Pola, Gina and Janina. They huddled together on their soiled eiderdown, their few possessions around them. Jozef kept an eye on the sacks carrying the horse collar and bicycle.

Resignation numbed the convoy. They travelled the remaining twenty-eight kilometres to Zharovski Posiolek, Vozhedgoski Forestry Collective, Vologda County. Their destination was a Gulag, a labour camp made up of rows of wooden barracks.

A man appeared with a list and directed them towards a hut. Without hesitation, Stasha asked him, "Are there any Polish men here?" He did not understand Polish. Stasha asked him again in Russian.

"No, you are the first Poles to arrive here."

Stasha turned to her children. "Tata's not here yet."

Janina was terribly upset to find that Irena had been taken to another camp for women only.

They learned that families from other osadas and villages in Eastern Poland had also been brought to this camp. They found that they too had been promised a reunion with their men. Had this been a lie to make prisoners more compliant? Stasha wanted to believe that Andrzej and the other men would join them soon.

The people imagined that nothing could be worse than the cattle trucks but they were wrong. Their new homes were poorly-constructed shacks made of sawn logs, hard earth and God-knows-what filling the gaps between the boards.

The arrivals, mainly families from three different osadas in Poland, were randomly assigned a part of a hut. The huts had a corridor running along one side where a single stove was situated. Short partitions at intervals acted as screens. They were overcrowded from the start.

"Mama, there isn't enough room for us all to sleep here," said Janina.

"It is better that we all sleep together. We'll keep each other warm," said Stasha.

"Yes, you'll see, we will soon be arguing over who has to sleep on the outside," said Jozef.

"There are lots of insects on this blanket," said Cheshek.

The family discovered that the entire place was riddled with lice. They at least had made a comfortable home, breeding profusely and pouring out of the cracks between the boards.

"These things are jumping all over my clothes," said Mietek in disgust.

Stasha whispered to him, "Just pretend that they are not there. I need you to be extra tough now for your little sisters."

There were no mattresses on the slatted wooden beds, just filthy old blankets that could practically move on their own. There was nothing to be done as their hunger, hopelessness and exhaustion took over and they lay down in their grim new abode, in their dirty clothes, and let the lice feed on them.

The next morning they awoke, disoriented. Stasha made an attempt to unpack some of their belongings. She was looking for a pan or the kettle. Their things were already riddled with lice. She wanted to put her head down and close her eyes again but she made herself tackle the situation.

Stasha went straight to the stove. Already there were women inspecting it.

"I'm Stasha Gwizdak. Can I help?"

A woman looked up. She said, "Stasha!"

"Lidia!" said Stasha, with relief. Lidia Czyz, her friend and fellow assistant from the nursery in Puzieniewicze, had arrived on another truck. The women clung to one another.

"Oh Stasha, what is happening? It's been like the worst nightmare imaginable."

"I know, and so many have already gone. How are you, Lidia?" Stasha asked.

"We had a terrible time getting here," said Lidia.

They broke their embrace and locked eyes. "The same with us," said Stasha.

"I'm so glad you are here," said Lidia. "We will do the best we can."

"Yes, we'll all pull together as we did back home," replied Stasha. "Now, we need to get this stove going."

"There's some wood we can use, over there." Lidia pointed to a pile in the corner.

A guard appeared at the door. "Everybody outside in half an hour."

"We can try to get this thing going and at least have a drink of hot water," said Lidia.

"People have packed things in newspaper and boxes. I'll gather some together. That should help to kindle the wood," said Stasha.

Soon, nearly everybody was huddled around the stove. Stasha had left Janina in charge of their allocated area, but the children were unsettled and cold and wanted to be near their mother.

When they assembled outside, Stasha coaxed the children into staying inside by the stove. There were a few other small children in the hut and, as with five and six-year-olds, everybody automatically became friends.

"Stasha? Stasha Gwizdak?" Stasha looked up to see another family from Puzieniewicze. They had been allocated a section at the end of the hut.

"Oh Stasha, my daughter is so poorly and we could feel a freezing draft all night. We are against two outside walls."

"Try not to worry. We can patch up the cracks. My sons will help to sort it out as soon as we are unpacked," said Stasha.

Outside, in the freezing cold, the guard announced, "No extra rations have arrived yet. There is only a small amount of bread per family." Hard, black bread was handed out.

The labour camp at Vorshega, like the many Gulags all over Russia, was just another component in a vast machine designed to support Stalinism. Hundreds of thousands of people were shovelled into a system of degradation, brutality and starvation. They were slaves, not expected to survive, only to support the war effort and raise up a mighty few. The anaemic Mother Russia was to be transfused with the spilled blood of old men, women and children.

Later that day, a camp official rounded everyone up for further instructions.

Guards were piling padded coats into a heap in a clearing outside one of the huts. "Take one bushlat each," they commanded.

Janina picked one out. "These are filthy." As she held it up, she asked, "What's this here? It looks like blood." She let it go and picked up another one. "This smells even worse. They have been worn before."

"Just grab some," said Jozef, worried that there might not be enough to go around. "We all need one. We'll be glad of these later. Nothing else will be warm enough here."

Benek was already wearing one as he passed another to

Mietek. Stasha and Janina fitted out Pola and Gina. With some comfort, they noticed that the smaller coats looked new.

"They are too big but we can put a tie round the middle", said Stasha.

That done, they reported to a hut to be given their work detail. Mama translated much of what was being said. This was a "corrective camp", although none of the Polish exiles could think what it was they were supposed to correct.

"Everyone over the age of thirteen will labour. You must work hard. No work, no food. Your ration is based on how much work you do. More work, more food. Simple."

Jozef, Janina and Benek, were to be taken into the forest to start their hard labour. Mietek and Cheshek were assigned duties around the camp. Mama would stay with the girls for now, as Pola had been sick all day.

Later that evening, it was abominably cold; water was frozen in the buckets inside the hut. Stasha checked Pola. The little girls were lying on either side of their mother. Pola's face was still burning.

"Is she all right, Mama?" asked Janina.

"She's settled now." As mother and daughter spoke, their breath came out in frosty clouds. The sick girl from their village had cried out for much of the night, keeping many of them awake.

"What is matter with her, Mama?" asked Janina.

"It looks like severe frostbite. The girl is in a lot of pain. What a sorry state we are in: the poor girl is suffering but people are annoyed with her because she is keeping them awake for a second night."

At six a.m. the following morning, Jozef, Benek, Janina along with many others, were transported into the forest on tractors and trailers driven by Ukrainian men. They learned that these men were the few survivors of the first group of prisoners to arrive at the camp. They had cut the wood and built the chalets in the most appalling conditions and the worst of the winter weather. The majority of them had died of exposure while sleeping in the open under the spruce trees before the first shelters were completed. They had been the first owners of the used bushlats.

The party was given their work detail. Jozef was handed a bow saw with instructions to fell trees. The trees would then be dragged into a clearing and sawn into specified lengths. Janina was instructed to strip bark from the logs. Benek, at only thirteen years old, would fetch and carry and act as messenger.

The work was very hard. Once the bark had been stripped, the wood was cut into three lengths, mainly for use as railway sleepers and boards. Logs with fewer knots would be sorted and reserved for use as pit props. Dragging the huge pine logs to the collection area was exhausting.

Jozef and Janina needed better gloves. Jozef's hand, injured on the cattle truck, had opened up again after just a few hours.

When they arrived back at the camp, Jozef went straight to the guard hut and surprisingly, strong, padded gloves were handed over.

"What did they say?" asked Stasha.

"The guard turned to his cronies and, from what I could make out, said, 'We have work targets and they must be met. So what do they do? They send us Osadniks, just a load of starving kids and their whining mothers.'" Jozef continued. Then he said, 'Here, take gloves and do the work of two.'"

"How was it in the forest?" asked Stasha.

"We managed, Mama," said Benek. "But everyone was dropping things because our hands were so cold."

"There were one or two accidents," said Janina. "Not too serious, but it is going to be difficult for some to work. Some people have already got deep cuts on their hands."

"Are you all right," asked Stasha.

"Just a few splinters, but I am glad of these gloves. Thanks brother," said Janina.

As they would soon find out for themselves, their work in the forests in winter was considered one of the worst jobs in the whole Russian Gulag system.

They had only been in the camp for a week or so before Stasha was laid low with the same burning fever as Pola. Cheshek was also having considerable problems walking. For the rest, at times, utter misery and hopelessness would prove to be as debilitating as any physical illness. They felt there was no excuse for feeling so wretched and negative when people around them were paying with their lives. Why did the walking well sometimes feel that there was no point in going on? Stasha wondered if they were all looking for an excuse to give in.

The young girl with frostbite had died during the night and her mother sobbed inconsolably.

Their food rations were paltry. Jozef could not do any more work than he had taken on, so their food rations could not be increased further. The basic ration, however, soon proved to be insufficient to live on. More problems started to occur when workers were too ill to go on or when it was too cold to work. Minus forty degrees was usually the limit. The workers were also expected to do no less than a twelve-hour day.

Although his knee was still troubling him, Cheshek volunteered to look after the small amount of livestock in the camp, which helped to bring in a little extra. Mietek set to work fetching and carrying water and helping to distribute the bread rations. Only six-year-old Pola and five-year-old Gina were exempt from work.

A few weeks after their arrival in the camp, a 'shop' was built. This was to be run by a Ukrainian couple. The shelves were practically empty but no one had money to buy anything anyway.

Stasha was often sick and troubled with dysentery. This sapped her strength and every day seemed harder. Nonetheless, she had the responsibility of being "dezhurnaya". This meant she had to stay behind and guard the belongings, look after the young and the sick in their barracks and act as general caretaker.

There were no medicines at all. Everyone suffered from stomach cramps caused by acute hunger. At times there was a little more food but even then they had to be careful, as they all learned to their detriment.

Someone had killed a small bear in the forest. It was cooked and shared around. The joy of having something substantial their stomachs turned to misery. Within the hour, they were all vomiting up the food. They could no longer cope with eating meat. They soon learned that if someone caught a rabbit and it went into the pot, they had to be very frugal and eat little morsels and make it last. Their bodies were weak with malnourishment and it was a great waste to vomit.

Personal hygiene was another impossible task. There was hardly ever any soap. When Janina managed to get hold of a small piece, it was rough, smelt like carbolic and left their hands sore.

They were all covered in infected fleabites and bites from other bedbugs. A particularly nasty infestation of red bugs dropped from the ceiling onto the bunks. When they were squashed, they gave out a putrid odour. Most of the children were also infected with scabies, adding to their discomfort.

The barracks reeked of dirty, mouldy, mildewed clothes. An open bucket (parasha) was used for those who had uncontrollable dysentery and the smell around this was abhorrent.

Stasha dragged herself up and tried to eat a piece of stale, black bread. She could not swallow, nor could she keep down the cold water. Her weight had dropped. She had never carried much on her bones to start with and now the weight loss and the lack of sustenance deprived her of any energy.

She was, however, insistent that she must go out and try and find something to supplement their diet. She left Mietek and Cheshek in charge of Pola and Gina and went out wearing the bearskin hat they had made. Nothing was ever wasted. Rabbit skins made slippers for the little ones. Needles and extra thread had been exchanged for spoons.

Meanwhile, in the forest, work continued until the weather took an alarming turn. Severe, unpredictable storms of this kind would often strike.

"Janina, where's Benek?" shouted Jozef. "There's a whistler coming!"

A wall of howling wind struck, blasting snow and ice into their faces, while churning the snow from the ground up into the air, causing a complete white-out.

Someone yelled, "Take cover!"

They were hardly able to see or breathe and hung on to one another and formed a chain in the hope that the person at the front was moving towards shelter. They only just managed to crawl beneath a trailer before snow completely covered them.

It was two hours before the blizzard relented. During roll call, two workers were discovered to be missing and a search was performed. Neither was found.

At the end of the day, Jozef, Benek and Janina arrived back at the hut. "Where's Mama?" Mietek had checked with the neighbours but no one had seen her. In a panic, the boys left the hut to ask around the camp.

Another hour passed. Pola started to cry and nervousness overcame the others. Gina, still regarded as the baby sister, would not acknowledge that her mother was missing. She repeated over and over, "Don't cry, Pola. Mama will be here soon."

Cheshek, struggling to walk but determined, returned. "No one can remember seeing her. Mrs. Czyz has been out looking for her too. Mama left before that horrible storm."

"Have you seen our Mama, Stasha Gwizdak?" They asked everyone they met and at last they found someone who had seen her earlier in the day.

"She sheltered in our hut while the storm was on but then said she must get back to the children," said a neighbour.

In desperation, Jozef and Benek decided that they must look further afield. However, the forest at night was pitch black and dangerous. Wolves, bears and wild boar roamed around but this was all the more reason for the brothers' determination to try, whatever the risks might be.

Suddenly Mietek's voice could be heard by almost the whole camp: "Mama! Mama!" Stasha was stumbling towards the clearing between neighbouring huts, supported by the shopkeeper. The brothers ran up to her and carried her back to the hut and laid her down. She was in a state of collapse.

Stasha was unable to eat and Janina could only persuade her to take sips of warm water. They had never seen their mother so ill and were fearful and panicky.

"What can I do for you, Mama?" asked Janina who noticed that her mother's skirt was soaking in bright, fresh blood.

Stasha managed to whisper, "Just a rest. I will be all right."

It was decided that, whatever the cost, Janina would not go to work the following day and instead stay and look after their mother. Jozef sought out the work administrators, as he knew this would incur penalties. He was told: "No work, no food. If she has another day off, you must report it or she may be sentenced to three months of hard labour."

In response, Jozef barked, "What the hell can this hard labour be? The work we are doing is killing us. How can a person work harder?"

"Quiet, you Osadnik! Or you will learn how hard things can really be." Jozef only just managed to keep his simmering temper under control.

Jozef and Benek worked like demons as their quota had to go further. Jozef spent his anger and resentment swinging his axe. Pola and Gina wanted to stay with their mother during the day but Janina now insisted that she had complete rest. Mrs Czyz looked after the girls.

After a few days, Stasha began to feel a little better but this only served to make her feel useless and frustrated. She had collapsed in the shop and had been taken in by the Ukrainian couple who did not know which hut she lived in. She had just managed to exchange a shirt of Andrzej's for an onion and a few potatoes.

A couple of days later, Mietek was out doing his duties, helping with the bread rations. As he left the bread depot carrying a tray, he tipped a loaf into the snow when no one was looking. Later, when he had finished his chores, he went back and retrieved the bread. He hid it under his coat and took it to his mother. With a pleased look on his face, he said, "Mama, this is for you. It will help you to get better."

Stasha scolded him. "Mietek, you must never do that again. It is stealing."

He looked so disappointed that Stasha added, "But you did it for the right reasons and for that, son, I am very grateful. You are a good boy." Knowing he had done it for her and the family so that they would not go so hungry, her heart went out to him. She slept with a warm feeling that night and she knew that she would soon be on the mend.

It was a Sunday morning and everyone had been given a day off. Stasha was up and about for the first time and her friend Lidia was having a hot drink with her.

"Stasha, I am glad to see that you are looking much better," said Lidia.

Janina was standing by the communal stove stirring a small pot; it was her own concoction made with some oatmeal. As she glanced across the hut she could see her mother and Mrs Czyz sitting and chatting. It warmed her to see them nodding and smiling until it dawned on her that the two women were just over forty years old. She shuddered, realising how much they had aged in such a short time.

Jozef appeared next to his sister.

"It does not taste too bad. There is only a spoonful each but it stays in your stomach longer than bread."

"Why do you get to lick the spoon to taste it, Janina?" asked Jozef.

"Cook's privilege, of course."

Jozef was furious. Lidia got up to go and Stasha walked across to join them. It saddened Stasha to see that hunger had driven her children to argue like that. Just the lick of a spoon caused anger and resentment.

"I am worried about Cheshek and his knee," she said. "He is hobbling around on it and it is obviously very painful."

"He never complains, Mama," said Janina.

"I know and that's worrying. I feel that he is keeping it to himself because things are so difficult. He must wonder if he will ever walk properly again."

"Do you think he needs something else to keep him occupied?" asked Jozef. "I think he needs some sort of interest, a responsibility, something he can call his own."

"Like what, Jozef? What do you have in mind?" Janina asked.

"I could sell the horse collar and buy a goat." There were a few animals in the camp, belonging to people who were there before they arrived. They were bred and young animals were occasionally for sale.

"I'll make a few enquiries."

"Yes Jozef, do that." Stasha felt slightly more positive.

Jozef bartered a good price for the collar and sold it to one of the officials. Some of the money went towards buying a female goat. Cheshek took charge of it with the aim of attempting to breed from it.

"We will have milk and that will give you children the calcium that your diet is lacking," said Stasha. Cheshek was delighted with his new acquisition and it soon became the family's pet..

11. 1941

A short summer

The thaw brought some relief from the unrelenting cold but the milder weather brought its own problems. Frostbite was replaced with midge and mosquito bites. One particular tick seemed to attack around the eyes and caused itching, swelling and smarting.

The camp community did not miss the cold but neither did the lice. Frost was one of the few ways to limit their spread. Clothes had been left outside to freeze and kill the lice. Now there was no way to eradicate them and they were present in ever-increasing numbers.

The poor diet and lack of nutrition were telling on everyone in the camp; all except the shopkeeper's wife who was a very large lady. The children made jokes about her when Mama was not listening (if she heard them they could still be rapped around their ears).

When the children whispered together, Mama knew just what was going on. Stasha would call out, "Miecyslaw, Apolonia, Reginka!" It was the only time they ever heard their full names.

"That is why the shelves are so empty, Mietek," said Pola.

"What, because she eats everything?" he replied.

"I want a shop, when I am big," said Gina. "Then I will

never be hungry again."

"I never see any food in the shop," said Mietek.

"She must eat it all at night when the shop is closed," said Pola.

The children were so very hungry and could not understand why the shopkeeper's wife was so fat. They ran away from her and would not speak to her when she addressed them. They were more used to seeing people with their bones sticking out.

The children were not alone out in their mistrust. With malnutrition rife, well fed-people attracted suspicion. Cheating, pilfering and prostitution were some of the methods adopted to escape death by starvation.

On one mild Sunday as they suffered from gnawing hunger, Stasha said to the children, "Let's go and see if we can find fruit or berries. It's the best time of the year to look. Mrs Swiercz found some bilberries the other day." They set out and collected as many as they could. For a few fleeting moments, it seemed like old times. They had the best day possible in their dreadful circumstances, spent together as a family. Even so, the treat of eating bilberries was followed by stomach pains and diarrhoea.

Food was still scarce and they had to supplement their diet with whatever they could find. Nettles were plentiful at this time of the year and they were quite palatable when made into soup.

On a daily basis though, they did not receive as many calories as their bodies demanded to perform the strenuous work. They were all beginning to look emaciated. Stasha and Janina no longer menstruated as a result of abnormal weight loss and malnutrition. Their faces were drawn and pinched. There was no toothpaste and no toothbrushes and plaque was building up on their teeth. Stasha worried about this, but the lack of sugar in their diet meant that, at least, no one was troubled with tooth decay.

Then typhus struck. Over the next few months, many

people fell ill and the death rate began to rise. Starvation had ravaged their immune systems, and their bodies had nothing left to fight the disease. Gastroenteritis was also commonplace and the first signs of a diet devoid of calcium and vitamin C were beginning to show. There were now cases of rickets and scurvy among the children in the camp.

Stasha was bathing her young daughters as best she could. Gina was standing in a bowl of warm water. Janina was on hand to dry her down as Pola waited her turn.

Janina saw the sores on Gina's body and mother and daughter couldn't help but notice Gina's legs, which were now just skin and bone, making her knees look proportionally greatly oversized. They averted their eyes before Gina noticed, and gave her a beaming smile. Stasha said, "Such pretty little girls you are."

They tucked them up and talked together out of earshot.

"Mama, I did not realise that the girls were in such a state."

"All the children have infected fleabites and scabies now," said Stasha. "There is nothing we can do to stop it. They itch so much, they scratch and scratch at night. That is how the diseases spread; they are flea-borne."

Mother and daughter were in exactly the same situation as the girls but they would have chosen to suffer more themselves if the little children could have been spared.

There was still no medicine in the camp. Scraps of news occasionally got through of the many battles being fought in Europe. No doubt the Russian Army got any supplies available and there was nothing to spare for the forgotten millions perishing in the labour camps.

The tractor men, whose job was to deliver the wood to other depots, brought in snippets of news. They, in turn, spoke to men from other areas and other camps. Whenever they got the opportunity, the family questioned them for news about Polish men. They now knew that there were many of these camps and hundreds of thousands of men, women and children had been deported from Eastern Poland and forced into hard labour. But there was never any news of their husbands and fathers.

In the Vorshega Camp, quite a few children were now left without mothers. One morning, on their way to work in the forest, they came across a sorry sight.

"Mama! Mama! Wake up, wake up." A little boy was crying and shaking his mother's open, rough coffin. They looked on helplessly as the boy was carried away, kicking and screaming.

"What will happen to him?" Janina asked the boy's neighbours.

"His mother has been ill for some time and he has been looked after by another couple. Their child died on the way here. They have taken him in. They will care for him as their own"

Such sights were now commonplace and the burial grounds were becoming as full of occupants as the camp itself.

Despair was now crushing any hope. Hunger was not only tormenting to the body but also the soul. Human dignity waned as people began to eye the piece of bread reserved for someone too ill to eat. Many began to hope that the morsel of food would soon be going spare.

Young children pleaded with hungry eyes while their mothers and grandmothers went with less. There was no such thing as selfishness when a body was fighting to stay alive. Self-preservation took over and a person could lose all inhibition. It was in this atmosphere that the fight for survival reached a critical point. The living conditions were now just the circumstances that surrounded each new death.

Mothers, bereft and grieving, felt misery and shame as they removed the shoes and coats from their children and parents as soon as they died. They had each been given only one padded jacket on arrival. Some of these were already well worn but there were no replacements except from the newly dead.

As children grew out of their clothes and shoes, or boots began to disintegrate, rope, string and rags were used to bind feet or repair broken footwear.

"This reminds me of the days back home when the White Russians had to bind their feet in rags and string. How the tide turns," said Stasha.

It was at this time that Stasha got down on her knees and prayed openly for the lives of her children. There was now almost nothing left. Just the week before she had sold the last article of Andrzej's clothing. This had upset her far more than she could justify and the feeling would not go away.

Stasha knelt with head bowed when a guard burst through the door. He grabbed her by the collar.

"It's against the rules. You know that," he barked. Stasha ignored his shouts and continued to pray loudly. Another guard appeared, alerted by the shouting, but Stasha had gone beyond reasoning. The guards pulled her to her feet. She was so light that she flew across the room and hit the floor.

"Get up. Get up! You know the rules and you know the punishment."

Praying was not allowed and she was dragged away and thrown into "The Hole". This was a dark, filthy, unheated hut. Former occupants had been locked in without toilet facilities and it stank like a pigsty.

Mietek was the first to return. Pola and Gina were huddled together crying. Mrs Czyz was taking care of them. "Your Mama has been taken away."

Without a word, this twelve-year-old boy ran to the place where his mother had been imprisoned. He tried to force open the lock. He could not move it. He began to kick the door.

"Mama, it's me, Mietek."

"Go back to the hut, son," said Stasha.

The door would not budge. He kicked and kicked at it.

People stopped and stood watching but no one dared to intervene or say a word.

With all his strength, Mietek kept going. "Mama, I'll get you out. Don't worry, Mama. I'll help you."

"Mietek, go back to the hut. Don't let them catch you. You'll be punished. Do as I say. Do you hear me?"

But the banging continued and slowly but surely the slats began to weaken and give way. Eventually the door split and Mietek broke it down.

Neighbours looked on. "We will all end up in trouble. Young Mietek's gone too far. Look at him, puffing and panting. His face is as red as borsch."

Mietek threw the bits of broken door over his shoulder and went into the punishment hut. He emerged holding his mother's hand. He did not say a word or make eye contact with anyone. He just marched his mother back to their barrack.

The family and everyone around them marvelled at his strength, a strength that seemed to come from nowhere. But they were worried and waited for some sort of retribution. Surprisingly, it never came. Not a word was ever said about the incident.

Autumn in Siberia

At the end of the summer, the prisoners were set to work haymaking. The hay was needed to feed the horses through the winter. They could earn a little extra food and rationing was not as bad.

Janina was playfully throwing hay over Benek and Mietek, when another work party arrived.

"Janina! Janina!"

Janina looked around, it was Irena. "Irena! Oh, Irena!"

They ran together and kissed and hugged.

"I am in a camp for women it is only a few miles from here."

"Perhaps I could visit on a Sunday? Said Janina. "Now I know where you are."

"Oh yes. Times are bad, aren't they my dearest friend?"

"But we are still alive and meeting you today is the best thing that has happened in a long time. How are you doing, Irena?"

"I miss my family terribly but all the women in my camp are on their own, so I mustn't complain. I am sure my family are alive and well somewhere but most of my new neighbours have lost all their family".

Following their reunion, the girls were able to meet-up again just once before the winter closed in.

The cold and dampness was creeping in fast. Over the last few weeks they had supplemented their rations with forest mushrooms. These were cooked in goat's milk and made a hearty soup. Other types of fungi were tried carefully. Stasha knew, although she could not remember how, that if you put a morsel of something on the inside of your bottom lip and it did not swell or react within a couple of minutes, it was edible.

Then Stasha fell ill again. Everyone in the hut was worried for her health and they all pulled together and helped where they could. Each time she succumbed to an infection, she failed to return to her previous level of health. She was failing. Janina and her brothers began regular searches of the camp to find anything to supplement their diet. They looked through the dustbins of the guards. In this, they were certainly not alone. Everyone was on the alert, watching for any waste to be dumped. The quickest got the bones, which would be boiled up to make soup, even if it just resulted in grey water. Any sustenance at all was of value.

When they first arrived at the camp, there were a few cats and dogs around the place. It was not a pleasant thing to contemplate, but every domesticated animal had now disappeared.

Jozef and Benek knew that they had probably eaten dog

meat. They were not happy about it but scruples had to be forgotten in order to survive. When anyone acquired anything edible in their hut, it was cooked and shared and no one asked any questions.

So fish bone soup with a few potato peelings was scraped together for Mama and she managed to sip it and keep it down. As always, she would not touch it until the children had soaked their morsels of stale bread first.

Weakened and painfully thin, Stasha managed to get off the wooden bed after a few days. Like all mothers, Stasha's problems were exacerbated by the fact that she fed her children before herself.

It was not part of her character to consider that she must help herself in an effort to be fit to help others.

Another Siberian winter

The body forgets pain and suffering to a degree. As women know, the world would be an emptier place if they had exact recall of natural childbirth. Equally, the prisoners found they had forgotten how cold a Siberian winter could be.

The residents of the camp were now more vulnerable and wasted than ever. Everyone was now suffering from night-blindness caused by malnutrition. They dreamt of food and their greatest wish in the world was to have enough to eat. They vowed that they would never again take food for granted.

Gone were any dreams of material gain. The attitudes of long ago seemed fickle and petty. Janina, now fifteen, did not dream of pretty dresses and shoes. What is a pretty dress on a starving, unwashed, emaciated body? But she still had her dreams and this helped her fight to survive. Her thoughts were fixed on the future, on "One day, I will..."

The hopes and wishes of the family were to be warm, well fed and all together again with Tata. Stasha prayed silently for the safety of her family every day. At times she thought that the situation was hopeless. "Oh Andrzej, where are you? Will we ever all be together again? How will you ever find us?" In these moments of despair, she pulled herself together, over and again.

"I must be positive. To give in at all will be my downfall. We have fought too hard and been through too much. But I have never felt so tired."

The Gwizdaks were awaiting the birth of a kid. Cheshek had done a good job looking after the goat and she was about to deliver. They had made a warm home for her in a dugout underneath the hut but the weather took a turn for the worse. Blizzards raged and it was now too dangerous for anyone to stay outside for long. With the help of his brothers, Cheshek managed to ensure that the goat was fed. The snow had drifted and created a barrier between the hut and the dugout and this made a snug nest.

After a couple of days, the storm abated and it was again safe to go outside. No living being could have survived more than fifteen minutes exposed to the elements. This was a risk that none of the community would take. They all knew of neighbours who had lost their lives caught outside when the blizzards hit.

Cheshek checked his goat. She had tried to get out. He limped back into the hut. They noticed that he seemed to be dragging his leg even more these days.

"Look at this! Everything here is bad, everything we do goes bad. I hate this place." Cheshek was holding two new-born kids. They had frozen to death.

"Cheshek, you have done your best, son. You could not have done more," said Stasha comfortingly.

"You still have the mother," said Benek.

"Yes, you could have lost them all," said Mietek. Pola nodded in agreement.

"Yes, good for you, Cheshek," and "Well done," said Jozef and Janina.

Although these words of support did not do much to appease Cheshek at the time, he reflected on them and after a short while, his resolve was to go on and try again. He had done his best and was glad that the mother had survived. From that day on, Cheshek developed a stronger constitution and hid his disappointments, seeming older than his years.

The family were now resigned to their situation and felt that any sort of luck had stopped short of the Russian border.

In fact, all of Stasha and Andrzej's children, and for that matter all of the other children in the camp, now possessed a precocious common sense and awareness. There was no point in whinging and complaining. Where before the children had cried out, now they wept only when there was a major tragedy.

The frozen kids were committed to the cooking pot.

12. MIETEK

Mietek confronted his mother: "Mama, I have the chance of some more work."

Stasha rested her weary bones and sat beside him, cradling his head. "What's this about, son?"

"I have been talking to one of the guards and he said there's a job I can do to earn extra bread."

"Doing what?"

"Er, just this and that. Sort of..." Mietek's words tailed off.

"What sort of this and that, Mietek?" Stasha could sense something was not quite right and she did not want Mietek being drawn into something unsavoury.

"Cleaning the latrines."

"Oh no. No, Mietek. Those latrines are filthy and disease-ridden. It's dangerous. The least time spent anywhere near them, the better."

"But Mama, I want to do my bit. I want to work and help like everyone else."

"No Mietek, I forbid it. There are regular outbreaks of typhus and cholera and it is too risky. No, and I mean no. Do not ask me again, do you hear me?"

Stasha's words fell on deaf ears and Mietek went ahead with the work. Benek and Jozef learned of Mietek's defiance and challenged him.

"I know I am younger but I am not stupid. I know we will all die here if we do not get any more to eat. You cannot work any more than you are now. I am the only one able to do any extra work. Mama forbade me to do it, but I know that I have no choice. I want to get out of here someday, just as badly as you do."

The brothers did not tell their mother about Mietek's new job. Stasha knew though, by the little extras that were now coming into the hut.

A few weeks passed and Stasha saw that Mietek was unusually quiet. He had been out of sorts for a few days but it was becoming more noticeable.

Janina and her mother sat on the wooden bunk, trying to burn lice from the children's blankets. "Mietek seems unwell, Mama, not like himself at all."

"I know, I have asked him if he feels unwell and he just says only like usual. I'm keeping my eye on him. I have told him he must stay in bed and rest."

It was difficult to tell if the children were suffering from what they could only describe as a feeling of a painful hole in their stomachs from hunger or if there was something else ailing them. The malnutrition they were all suffering brought many different symptoms, including swollen stomachs, dizziness and severe headaches.

Stasha had noticed that the hair on her head was thinning while her body hair was increasing. She tried to hide it, as she did not want to worry Janina. Whatever situation a young woman might be in, the loss of their hair would upset them terribly. Janina, however, had realised why her mother had taken to covering her head with a scarf.

Meanwhile, Mietek was not improving. On closer questioning and further coaxing, Mietek said he felt the same as ever but just a bit worse. But he was so quiet, hardly speaking a word, which was so unlike himself and this disturbed them all.

Stasha did not know what to do. Their rations had been almost non-existent for the last few days. Even though so many people had died, they were not receiving the same rations as usual. She walked into the woods, just a short distance from their camp, and searched for anything that could be edible. She found some greens and in her desperation she took them back and cooked them.

The children tried to eat the greens but within an hour they were all retching and vomiting. Stasha vomited blood and had to lie down. Lidia Czyz came to see what was happening and tried to help.

"What has happened? What is the matter?" asked Mrs Czyz.

Pola came forward and offered an explanation. "Mama tried to cook grass, we had nothing else. It made us all sick and made our stomachs hurt just the same as it hurts when we have nothing to eat."

Mrs Czyz and her family were starving just like everyone else. "What have we been driven to? What sort of a world is it, where mothers cook grass to try to stop their children dying of hunger?" she cried.

This alien community, sick and wretched, dressed in flea-infested rags and many with rag-bound feet, had reached a new low point. As time went by, none of them would ever forget that day when they were starving, and Mama tried to feed them cooked grass.

Mietek's condition was worsening. His right leg was red and swollen. Stasha and Janina nursed him as best they could but he was not responding.

He developed a raging fever and they sat with him through the night. Although it was freezing cold, he was burning hot and nothing they did would bring his temperature down. After a couple more days, Mietek stopped eating altogether.

It was a great surprise when one of the chief administrators sent a message to say that permission had been granted for Mietek to be taken to the nearest Russian hospital some twenty-six kilometres away.

"I don't want him to be away from us," Stasha addressed all her children, "but I know it is for the best."

"Don't let Mietek go, Mama. Tata had to go away and he didn't come back," said Gina.

At that moment a guard arrived at the hut and spoke to the family. "There has been a discussion between some of us and we approached the head to ask if he would consider special arrangements in Mietek's case. He is a good lad and some of us want him to be given a chance of better treatment. We will help as much as we can. A cart will arrive later today to take him but they will not allow any of you to go with him. One of us has volunteered to take him."

Stasha wrapped Mietek up as well as she could. "They have medicines at the hospital. You will get better soon, son."

Mietek managed to say, "Yes, Mama."

When the guard came to carry him out, Stasha recognised him as the man who had put her into solitary confinement as a punishment for praying. He had witnessed Mietek breaking down the door and rescuing his mother. They all remembered that there had been no punishment for his actions.

Stasha felt helpless at not being able to go with him but knew he would receive the best treatment available. She thanked God for this mercy. Another of her prayers had been answered.

Jozef, Benek and Janina were all struggling badly, but they had to work just as hard as ever. No matter how tired they felt, they were just as dependent on their rations as before. They would trudge to the forest and work a long day once more consumed with the heady smell of pine resin.

A few days following Mietek's admission, Stasha, sick with worry, decided to ask for permission to visit him in hospital. She knocked on the door of the administrator's office.

"Come in."

The administrator did not look up and carried on writing in his book. He was ignoring her. She was annoyed with herself for even contemplating this request.

"What do you want?"

"My son is ill in hospital in Vologda. May I go and see him?" asked Stasha.

"It is Sunday tomorrow. You may go then. Only two of you, no more."

The following day Stasha and Jozef set out, marching silently and purposefully with heads down, along the only road leading out of the camp to the nearest town.

In all the time they had been in the camp, nearly eighteen months, they had only left it as part of a work party. They had never been so far and it had begun to feel as if there was no world outside the labour camp. They did not dwell too much on any of this, as they were desperate to get to see Mietek.

They continued mile upon mile along the track made by years of pine logs dragged by tractor and trailers; a by-product of their hard labour. The scenery was unchanging pine forests all the way but, although monotonous, their journey seemed short.

Jozef approached a local man and asked directions and they soon found the hospital. They rounded the building, found the entrance and went in. There was a desk on one side of a reception hall. Stasha and Jozef reported to the female clerk.

Immediately they noticed how run-down and shabby the hospital was. There was a pungent smell of carbolic soap and cheap disinfectant, struggling to mask the stink of urine. They were told to take a seat in an area just off the entrance. The room was dank, with black mould on the walls. The floor was filthy. There were distant sounds of hacking coughs and retching, mingled with rambling voices. Stasha tried to block out the noise. She stared around the room. There was a sink in one corner. She noticed that it had a large piece chipped out of it. A tap dripped constantly and a long brown stain indicated the route of the water. Blackened grout crisscrossed the cracked, white tiles.

A pleasant young man in a white coat came for them. "This way, please."

As they followed him, he said, "We struggle here. We have few staff and few resources, but we do the best we can."

As they entered a ward, Jozef's attention was drawn to a man lying totally immobile and covered to his chin with a thin sheet. He quickly averted his eyes. The man in the bed looked skeletal with jaundiced, loose skin covering his sunken face. His jaw gaped, as if the strength to close his mouth was too much to muster. Inside his mouth, his teeth had been reduced to sparse, black stumps. Scurvy and the stinking rot of caries had worked like pliers on his gums. There were deep indentations in his temples at the side of lifeless eyes, another sign of malnutrition, now easy to recognise. Jozef thought that he had seen many a dead person who looked ten times better than this poor man.

This was someone's son, brother, maybe a father. Why is one human life not valued as much as the next? Jozef felt appalled by the injustice of a world that measured action or degrees of empathy on race or perceived social status.

They arrived at Mietek's bed and Mama kissed him and held his hand. She whispered in his ear as she stroked his hair, which was damp and matted.

Jozef told him, "Hurry up and get well, little brother. Everyone is missing you. It's too quiet."

Mietek, still looking pale and weak, only spoke a few quiet words but he managed a smile for his Mama. "Take care, my son. Get better and you will be back with us again in no time."

Stasha had to drag herself away. She had not thought how hard it would be to leave him there. He looked so helpless and much smaller than she remembered. They had to get back before dark and they waved until they could see him no more. He gazed towards them as long as he could see them.

A few days passed. Each day rolled into the next. Now there was something to look forward to. The family was incomplete and they could hardly wait for Mietek to come back. Pola and Gina thought what tales he would have to tell. Nothing ever happened to them and he had been somewhere different. They had no concept of how ill he had been and it was a good distraction to imagine his adventures.

Stasha was about to ask for another visit when an official told Jozef that he and his mother could go to the hospital and visit Mietek again.

Stasha and Jozef set out to walk the twenty-six kilometres. Stasha felt uneasy. Had his condition worsened? She was determined to keep her spirits up and was content enough to be allowed to visit her son. At least if he was feeling well enough to eat, there would be food at the hospital.

This time the journey seemed to take forever, but eventually they arrived. At first, no one seemed to know anything. He had been moved. There was a lot of whispering and asking around. Eventually, someone came forward and led them into a room. From there they were led through another door and saw the same young doctor standing next to a table. On it lay Mietek, covered with a blanket.

The doctor stepped forward and spoke to them in Russian, a language that was now familiar to Jozef as well as his mother. "I am so sorry, he has already gone."

The room spun and the walls began to collapse in on Stasha. She felt as if she was being asphyxiated and fell to her knees. Jozef stooped and tried to help her to her feet. Her legs would not support her. Jozef had to leave her in a crumpled heap. She was trembling and the blood had drained from her face.

Jozef wanted to hit something or somebody or both. He could no longer contain his anger. "No! No more. Enough.

I've had enough of this shit. They've put my brother in his grave!" He leaned over Mietek's emaciated body. "Mietek, little brother." He turned on the doctor. "You Ruskis have killed him. What did he ever do to you? What did he ever do to anyone? He is only a boy and you bloody Bolsheviks have killed him!"

Until this moment, Stasha had not made a sound. She had stayed on the floor, frozen. She raised her voice. "Jozef, stop. You will be arrested if you continue." She dragged herself onto her feet and squared up to Jozef. "Be quiet now, Jozef. Just be quiet. Don't make me lose two sons in one day." Jozef managed to catch her before she collapsed again. She was able to stay upright with the support of her eldest son.

Security guards rushed to the door in response to Jozef's shouts, but the young doctor waved them away. This was either out of understanding for their loss or a lack of knowledge of the Polish language. Later, on reflection, it was comforting to believe the former was the case.

Stasha propped herself up against the table and said a prayer over her youngest son's body. She kissed him and held his hand, which was now cold. She whispered to him and stroked his hair, something she had always done. She remembered with such fondness, through her tears, how this would always settle him as a baby.

Jozef kissed his brother for the last time and letting go, gave into the sobs that wracked his body. Although he was now a young man, there was no embarrassment to his distress. Jozef's grief was inconsolable. He was now the man he would always be: a man of hard certainties. He had promised his father that he would take care of the family and, as far as Jozef was concerned, he had failed Mietek.

His mother drew back the blanket to take a last look at her young son. They saw that his frail body had been cut from his chin to his waist and roughly sutured.

The doctor then spoke and tried to explain that Mietek had suffered internal problems that led to peritonitis. From what they could decipher, he said that blood poisoning had taken the boy. But his mother and brother knew that Mietek, who had been such a strong boy, had died from unhealthy conditions and starvation.

Stasha walked the twenty-six kilometres back to the camp. It could have been two hundred kilometres; she did not want to arrive anywhere. She was living a nightmare. She felt that as long as they remained silent, this terrible thing might not have happened.

Then, in an instant, the reality of her loss overcame her. She saw that one way or another, this place would take them all.

Jozef took his devastated mother's arm and they began walking again. Stasha sought out her God, who seemed more distant than ever. She believed that evil was trying to reign here. Was God too distracted by his almighty battle to drive out the devil raging throughout Europe?

Stasha prayed silently all the way back. God, give me strength to get through another day. I just want to die, but I must live for the rest of my children. I feel destroyed. I do not know if I can go on.

No one knows how Stasha found the strength to walk to the churchyard a week later. Only she and Jozef were allowed to attend Mietek's burial. So many graves had been dug and more holes waited, like hungry, gaping mouths waiting to be filled.

Mietek's rough box was placed in the ground and Stasha silently prayed for his soul and then spoke quietly. "I know there is no cross, nothing to mark your grave, but know this: there is a mark in my heart, a cut so deep that I will always bear the scar and always feel it. I will never forget you. Goodbye Miecyslaw, my beautiful boy. Until we meet again, may God bless you and keep you." As she continued to pray, a glimmer of light appeared as a voice in Stasha's head spoke. "Mietek is now with Leonia and they are both in God's hands." Stasha's faith was her lifeline. Her God gave her the strength to go on when others in her situation would have given up.

Nothing more can be said of the grief and pain of Mietek's death. No words are profound enough. The sadness caused by this tragedy would be carried by all the Gwizdaks for the rest of their lives.

Quite a few weeks passed and Stasha was at last able to smile as she shed tears for her lost son. She remembered all of his wonderful qualities. She would never forget what he had done for her and how he had shown his affection. How proud she was of her young son and how grateful she was to have been blessed with him for his short life. "Only twelve years," she thought. "That was all we had."

Stasha felt so alone. She had her children, and Janina was a great support to her but she needed Andrzej. He did not even know that he had lost a son.

Christmas 1941 was equally as miserable as the year before. The older children told the younger ones that Father Christmas did not know where Russia was.

However, Jozef and Benek had uprooted a small fir tree and brought it into the barrack. Stasha and the children decorated it with bows made from little bits of coloured rags and little stars made from paper.

Sadly, as Christmas Day did not fall on a Sunday, everyone had to go to work..

13. 23ᴿᴰ FEBRUARY 1942

Liberation

Almost two years had passed while the family lived as slaves and prisoners in the labour camp, when news filtered through of Operation Barbarossa.

The Nazis had turned on their ally and begun an assault on Russia. No doubt similar treachery had also been part of Stalin's greater plan but Hitler had made his move first.

Churchill and Roosevelt were quick to make a pact with Stalin for a united force to crush Hitler's regime. One of the conditions of this agreement was to grant amnesty to all Polish Nationals held on Russian soil.

The word 'amnesty' was not acceptable to the exiled Poles, as it would only be an appropriate term for prisoners of war. The hundreds of thousands of Polish nationals forcibly exiled were not prisoners of war. They were ordinary people transported to Russia as slave labour.

However, the Western Allied governments were treading a fine line and needed the utmost co-operation of the tyrant. They were not in a position to argue over terms, although they were fully aware of Russia's autocratic leadership. Stalin succumbed to international pressure and agreed to allow all Polish-born people to leave Russian soil.

The Gwizdak family had to find their own way across

Russia, avoiding war zones. Their plan was to make their way to Persia (Iran), one of the few countries that had offered them temporary asylum. The fact that Persia had opened its doors and its arms to refugees and its generosity at this time would never be forgotten by the Polish people who passed through. They would find themselves on the receiving end of overwhelming aid and support.

News reached Jozef, Janina, Benek and Cheshek that General Anders was lobbying to recruit a Polish Free Army to fight alongside the allies. Although they were not fit to fight, as they were barely able to stand, they were determined to try to find transport to the Middle East. However, General Anders did not wait for confirmation and began his recruitment immediately. At the last moment, Jozef collapsed. He was diagnosed with typhus and carted off to the hospital twenty-six kilometres away where Mietek had died.

The exodus began. Everything was in a state of confusion and everyone was overwhelmingly anxious to get out as soon as possible. Stasha was still mourning Mietek, which was doing nothing for her already precarious health. Now she had the added worry of leaving Jozef behind, with no way of knowing how he was.

Red Cross parcels arrived at the camp. Stasha was given a large, square box.

"Two pairs of ladies' shoes," she said to Janina. "I will try to sell these to help with our journey."

Exit permits were issued to the evacuees and documents distributed to allow them rations to support them on their way. Stasha and the children planned to travel with Lidia Czyz. They acquired a little extra bread over the last few days and dried some in readiness for their journey.

Stasha noticed the poor condition of Lidia's feet.

"I have difficulty walking due to the frostbite, Stasha," said Lidia.

The bloodied rags covering Lidia's feet were falling off.

"Can we bind them a little better?" she asked.

"I can't stand the pressure of the string. The sores are too deep," said Lidia.

"You will never manage to walk out of here like that."

Stasha knew that a pair of shoes could mean a train ticket or a precious meal, but she gave a pair of green shoes to Lidia, who could not find the words to thank her friend. They just hugged one another. Stasha sold the remaining pair to the stationmaster at Vologda.

All families but one, too ill to move, left the labour camp. The atmosphere was hopeful but there was also a lot of trepidation. Many were so weak that they had difficulty walking and the jubilation they expected to feel was now replaced by uncertainty. They would not feel safe until they had left Russia.

Jozef had indeed been left behind and was in a state of panic in the rat hole of a hospital. He had been delirious when he arrived but was now improving, only to discover that he was in the place where his young brother had died. This did not have the effect that might be expected; as he improved he felt as if Mietek was close by and this comforted him.

Jozef watched as one by one the patients around him died and were wheeled out. He felt that he had improved somewhat and feared that if he stayed much longer, he would catch another disease and he too would leave in a box.

Most of the convoys heading for the Middle East had now begun their long journey to the eastern borders of Asia, to avoid the war raging in Europe. Jozef knew that time was running out. He heard rumours that Stalin was about to go back on his word and close the Russian borders. With a feeling of foreboding, he prepared to go whether he was fit or not. However, once out of bed, he realised that he was not as able as he had hoped. This was where fate took over, brought on by his own careless actions.

During the night, he took a piece of bread from a man

who has just died in the next bed. After two years of starvation, Jozef was thrown into panic whenever he saw a bit of food going to waste. As he did not need it, he traded it for a cigarette. Then he was caught.

"You steal bread from a dead man just to buy a cigarette. Get out of this hospital," ordered a charge nurse. Jozef was kicked out.

This action was to save him from a terrible fate. Jozef only just managed to join the penultimate convoy out of Russia. What he had heard was correct. Stalin would soon stop the convoys and announce that anyone left on Russian soil was now a Russian citizen. Any Polish men left, although many were barely able to stand, would be forced into the Russian army.

Moreover, any orphaned Polish children remaining in Russia (of which there were many) would have to stay there and grow up without knowledge of their true identity and nationality.

Miraculously, Jozef managed to catch up with the rest of his family and they all travelled together.

It would now take many months and thousands of miles to wind their way toward a meeting point in Tashkent. Once again, troop transport took precedence. There was much stress and anxiety at each step of the journey and they were all sick with worry that they might be prevented from going further. Many hundreds of people were gathered at every station along the way. Some told stories of having walked hundreds of kilometres in a few days to reach a train to take them south and to the Middle East.

The children were all understandably nervous, as their last train journey had brought them to a living hell. They persisted in asking their mother, "Where are we going? What will it be like? Will Tata be there this time?"

Stasha consoled them as well as she could.

"It will be warm and sunny and I will make sure that you will never be hungry again. Now don't worry, my little ones, happy times are coming very soon."

They were not easily appeased though, as nothing had improved in any great measure since they had left the camp. The stories they heard of human endurance and determination helped to lift their spirits and feed the minds that had stagnated and almost given up hope during the two years of suffering and imprisonment. It soon became apparent that some of the labour camps, out in the far north reaches of the Arctic Circle, yielded very few survivors. On one of the many train journeys, Stasha, her children and their friends and neighbours were joined in their coach by a couple of men.

One was a young man who was dreadfully disfigured. Part of his face was blackened and his nose was almost completely gone. His hands were also black and he was missing some fingers. His bare feet were swollen and ulcerated. The stench was almost unbearable, but the women felt overwhelming pity and compassion. They shared their few morsels of food with the men, who had nothing. The other man spoke; the young, disfigured man remained silent. He took the hard bread and nibbled it like a mouse and only looked up to glance around furtively as if someone would try to take it from him.

The older man, dressed in rags and with matted hair and grey beard, talked with the refined voice of a wealthy, educated Pole. "We have been incarcerated in one of the camps in the far north. We are among the very few who made it out alive. Most men died from the bitter cold, hunger and exhaustion within weeks of arriving. These Gulags are arctic killing fields where men last a few months at most. The turnover of flesh was unbelievable. Hundreds continually arrived as hundreds more were shovelled into pits."

He went on to explain that it seemed that only the very fittest lasted a little longer. The young man had been a champion athlete at his university. He was now not only diseased and very weak, his mind had gone.

The older man told them that he had lasted longer because of things he had done that he would never forget and never forgive himself for; and neither, he feared, would God.

Janina looked down and noticed that he had made his own shoes. He was wearing pieces of rubber tyre, with wire treaded through, tied to his feet with rope.

The women, tired and listless, still managed to gather strength to ask the all-important questions they would put to everyone they met: "Have you seen or heard word of any Polish Army Officers during the last two years? Were there any in your camp? Who have you spoken to? What did they know?" Stasha was desperate for news of Andrzej. Just some news, any word at all.

She had to see him before he re-enlisted and was sent away to fight again. No one seemed to have any news of their men and this was very disheartening. They were all praying for information.

The group was to witness many unspeakable and sickening things on their long journey east and then south to Tashkent, skimming the borders of China and Afghanistan on their way to Persia. During this journey back, like the journey over two years before, people began to lose the fight to stay alive.

It was sad to see people who had survived through so much die now that there was a chance of freedom. They would collapse and be unable to get up. They were left where they fell by their friends and families, who had no alternative but to carry on without them. The fallen had no food, shelter or aid. Many would never meet again or learn each other's fate.

They now had to hold on and try to survive long enough to complete their journey. They dreamed constantly of food, warm food and the warm sun on their faces. Repeatedly, their dreams of better days were extinguished as they stopped at station after station where bodies of men, women and children were unloaded and piled on the platform. The corpses were so ragged and bare that there was little of use to the refugees.

After a few months of travelling, the Gwizdak family arrived in the Russian port of Krasnovodsk on the Caspian Sea. Here, the extent of the mass exodus from labour camps all over Russia became apparent.

Thousands of people arrived daily. The scene was on an epic scale: so many poor souls, emaciated, ragged and shoeless, a sea of beggars.

They arrived in blistering sunshine and were taken to a building set up as a registration post.

After a period of gradual introduction to food and some time to rest, Stasha and Janina started to look for temporary work. They found jobs in the huge laundry service set up to deal with both army and civilian needs.

Pola and Gina had to stay in an orphanage that had been set up to cope with the many children who had been separated from their families. It would eventually be discovered that many of these children had lost their entire family.

Gina and Pola were not happy about their accommodation. After a few days, Pola said, "Come on Gina, I have wrapped up some bread and we are going to walk until we find Mama and Janina." The girls set out.

It was getting dark and they seemed to have been walking for a long time. Gina started to cry and Pola was afraid that they would get lost. In the end they walked quietly back to the orphanage, feeling totally defeated.

A sea of tents now lined the shoreline as people waited their turn to be shipped across the Caspian Sea to Persia.

Order started to appear from the chaos, as men, irrespective of whether they were fit or not, had only one wish: to join General Anders' Army and fight for a free Poland. This was also the only sure way to secure a ticket out of Russia.

Janina applied to join the WAF and was to be accepted if her health improved and she managed to gain weight. Nothing would stop her and it was only a matter of time as far as she was concerned.

Benek lied about his age. He was still only sixteen, but claimed to be eighteen. He would have to wait and see.

Cheshek had been hospitalised for his knee wound. The surgeon reported that if there was no significant improvement within a few weeks, he would have to amputate the boy's leg.

Pola and Gina had to stay in the orphanage while their mother worked in the laundry. Stasha could hardly bear to be apart from them, but they needed to recover and regain their health. She consoled herself with the fact that it would not be long now before they would receive their passage to cross the Caspian Sea and leave Russia forever.

It was Easter Sunday, 1942, in Krasnovodsk and Stasha had managed to get hold of some eggs. She boiled them with onion skins to colour the shells. This was a tradition from back home in Poland.

She took them to the hospital and, although she could not go into Cheshek's room because of quarantine and infection control rules, she smiled at him through the window.

Cheshek saw Mama holding up the eggs and they waved at each other. Easter eggs, from that day on, would always be very special to him. Stasha allowed herself to believe that better days would be coming soon.

She learned that she, Pola and Gina were to travel to Masindi in Africa to stay in a refugee camp run by Catholic nuns for the duration of the war.

Jozef attempted to enlist but approval was dependent on his health improving. Like everyone else, he was suffering from malnutrition and scurvy, although he had managed to keep all his teeth, but weakness and night blindness were causing him problems. He was also worried that the poor eyesight in his left eye would be discovered.

Benek had been found out. He was called to the recruitment office.

"We have a problem with your date of birth. We have two records, one stating that you are sixteen and another that you are eighteen. We also have another listing here for someone I believe is your brother, Jozef, with the same birthday. Can you explain this? You are not twin brothers, are you?"

"Yes sir, we are twins."

It was obvious to the officer that Benek was trying to pull a fast one. However, he appreciated that the young lad was so desperate to get away and that joining the forces was his only chance. He would do anything to be accepted. It would be a while before he would see any action as, like the other recruits, Benek would need time for care and nourishment to bring him back to a reasonable standard of health. The recruiting officer changed the records to show that Jozef and Benek were twin brothers. Benek was enlisted in the Polish Air Force Cadets.

Stasha was in poor health again and she often felt very weak. During her time in Russia, she had been unable to recover completely between bouts of infection. This had taken its toll and she could not imagine that she would ever regain her full fitness. She told herself that she must continue to improve. It was only a few weeks until they were to travel to Africa. While she wished that day to dawn as soon as possible, Stasha was still desperate for news of Andrzej. No one had heard anything yet and she dreaded the thought of leaving without hearing of him.

Many of the families, those in their labour camp and many who had arrived from others, were seeking their menfolk. Tens of thousands of families arrived daily and as yet there was still no word of them. They could only pray that their husbands and fathers had not been among those sent to such camps as Vorkuta or Kolyma beyond the Arctic Circle where even the guards were said to perish in no time at all.

Jozef faced his final check. He still had a long way to go before he was fit, but based on his progress and a good prognosis, he would be well enough to travel within the next few months. On this assessment he was accepted into the First Polish Paratrooper Training Corps. He now joined his fellow comrades in the camp set up on the outskirts of the province.

A week before they were due to depart for Africa, Stasha went to see Jozef one last time. She had heard that he was accepted for Paratrooper training and was building up his strength. She walked to the tent village and sought him out.

They spoke very little but their eyes said everything.

"Mama!" Jozef kissed and hugged his mother. He felt her bones through her thin clothes. She had brought him some milk, a delicacy to them and still scarce.

As she gave him the milk, she remembered cradling him, her first-born child for the first time, a tiny scrap of humanity in her tired arms. Now he was a man and was to become a Polish Paratrooper.

"We have come a long way. I am so proud of you, Jozef. Fight for your country and when we meet again the world will be a better place. Take care and come back to us safely."

She had to let him go. She had done her best. She walked away and Jozef watched, noticing how frail she had become. She turned back so they could wave until they finally lost sight of one another.

"Who was that, Joe?" asked a new friend and comrade.

"That was my Mama," replied Jozef and turned his head to hide his vulnerability as his emotions threatened to overwhelm him. He was to be mobilised very shortly and did not know when they would meet again. It had been explained to them all that intensive training would take place as soon as their physical strength allowed. Their location and training was to be a secret and from then on no one would be allowed to know their whereabouts.

14. EXODUS

Fear and dread gripped the refugees once more as they heard that Stalin was starting to close the borders and would not allow any more Polish nationals to leave Russia. It was confirmed that anyone left on Russian soil would officially become a Soviet citizen. Any able-bodied men would fight in the Red Army. Stasha prayed that Andrzej and the rest of the men had managed to get out.

Plans were made to transport all troops and refugees to Persia. Passenger lists were drawn up for places on ships to cross the Caspian Sea to Pahlavi. The ships were nothing more than rusty tubs but the refugees were grateful for anything that would take them away from Russia.

Gina, Pola and Stasha would be the first to go. They would be met in Pahlavi by members of the Red Cross and from there they would receive safe asylum in camps for displaced persons in British Commonwealth countries.

Just a few days before they were due to leave, Stasha collapsed and was taken to a nearby hospital only semi-conscious. She was suffering from diarrhoea with haemorrhaging and, it was discovered, malaria. The girls had to leave and their Mama was to join them on a later crossing. Jozef and Janina were leaving on separate convoys a few days apart.

Benek called at the hospital to see Cheshek. The doctor in charge sought Benek out and informed him of his brother's condition. "TB has severely damaged the knee joint. There are only two outcomes. There is an infection in an old wound and gangrene could set in. He needs an operation now or he will lose his leg. The recommended procedure in this case is surgery that to save his leg but he will never have full flexibility in it again. There will also be some muscle wastage, therefore I cannot promise he will have much movement in his leg in the future."

As Mama was in another hospital, there was no one else to give consent for Cheshek's operation. Benek, underage but pretending to be eighteen, had only one thought: we have got this far, we can't give up now. Cheshek must survive. He must have the surgery. Benek signed the form. Cheshek had his operation and was transported across the Caspian Sea on a boat leaving with stretcher cases.

Stasha, still weak but with no time to lose, was only just able to leave the hospital to join her friend Lidia Czyz on the penultimate crossing.

Benek would sail on the very last convoy.

Stasha was not really well enough to travel but the borders were now closed and she would be left stranded, so she had no choice. She desperately wanted to be reunited with Pola and Gina. She knew they would be fretting and worried. The boat she was travelling on was crammed full of men, woman and children; many becoming sick, some already sick when they arrived on board. Nevertheless, the air was cleaner and fresher and a look of hope began to appear on many a face. What a sorry sight they made: a crowd of ragamuffins, still half-starved, but some with tans that gave them the illusion of better health.

At the quayside in Pahlavi (Anzali), the refugees disembarked, many of them barely able to walk. It was a moving scene: men and women in their thousands fell down on their knees and kissed the ground, thanking God for their liberation.

Benek arrived in Pahlavi, knowing that his family had been evacuated before him. As yet, no one had any news of the whereabouts of their father and his comrades. The family could only hope that they had been evacuated at another time or place.

A makeshift city comprising more than two thousand tents, provided by the Iranian Army, had been hastily erected along the shoreline of Pahlavi. It stretched for several miles on either side of the lagoon, a vast complex of bathhouses, latrines, disinfecting booths, sleeping quarters, bakeries and a hospital. Every unoccupied house in the city was requisitioned, every chair claimed from local cinemas. Still, the facilities were inadequate.

The Iranian and British officials who watched the Soviet oil tankers and coal ships list into the harbour on 25th March 1942 had little idea how many people to expect or what physical state they might be in. Only a few days earlier they had been alarmed to hear that civilians, women and children, were to be included among the evacuees, something for which they were totally unprepared.

The ships from Krasnovodsk were grossly overcrowded. Every available space was crammed with passengers. Some of them were little more than walking skeletons, many were still covered in lice, some fiercely clutched bundles of their precious few possessions, but most were barefoot with nothing but the scant rags they stood up in.

The refugees' first sight was an endless field of tents. They were greeted by wonderfully efficient teams of British female volunteers. Very organised, friendly and helpful, the women handed out soap and towels and directed people to delousing centres.

Complete sets of clothes were distributed and all the old clothes were burned. It was decided unanimously between these women that the practice of shaving children's heads to prevent re-infection by lice should only happen once and not be repeated: these children had been through enough. Along with their mothers, they had suffered the most appallingly inhumane conditions and should now be treated with great gentleness. Their hair was sign of their individuality and freedom. They were no longer prisoners and should not be made to feel differently.

What could not be expressed enough was the gratitude felt by the Polish refugees to the Iranian people. More than food and shelter, the refugees needed warmth and friendship to begin to rebuild their lives and this was given generously.

As the evacuees arrived in their thousands, the British authorities who were monitoring the situation were dumbstruck. A shocked member of the British Red Cross approached the officials after another wave of arrivals and said, "What the hell is going on here? Where are all of these people coming from?"

"We are receiving hundreds of orphaned children every day. Some of them have walked hundreds of miles on legs that don't look strong enough to hold them up," said one of the officials.

"Where from?"

"Russia. From labour camps. They tell us that they are only the few who managed to survive and get out before Stalin closed the borders. They were imprisoned for over two years. They tell us that they were taken away in cattle trucks in their thousands during the winter of 1940, in mass convoys. It seems that this went on for some months. They were dispersed to labour camps all over Russia. Every family reports having lost a mother, sisters or brothers. Many say their husbands have been missing since 1939."

"God in heaven!"

At this point, Stalin's horrific treatment of the Polish race was unknown to the rest of the world.

Jozef was walking back to join his battalion when he started to feel very unwell. He put this down to the fact that he had bought two pears and eaten them quickly. His stomach still could not take very much and certainly not the kind of food he had not eaten for years. The fruit had looked so good that he could not resist. He walked a little further but he started to feel worse. His head was spinning. His legs gave way and he blacked out.

Back at the base, no one could find him. After a few hours, a search party was sent out. Jozef had collapsed and had been found unconscious behind some outhouses. He was admitted to hospital with malaria.

Benek heard by chance that Jozef was in the fever hospital. He had been searching desperately for his brother. He had to leave soon as he had been ordered to stay in a convent in Haifa to convalesce and rebuild his health. By the time he found him, Jozef was up and managing to walk a little.

Jozef saw Benek coming towards him and raised his hand. He knew from his brother's expression that something was terribly wrong. Fear started to rise in his gut. As they came together, Benek's usual bear hug was lacking in strength and Jozef felt the slump in his brother's shoulders.

They both sat down on the edge of the bunk. What had happened? One look at his brother and he knew he was completely broken. Benek tried to speak. His eyes filled and overflowed. Jozef knew that this was bad, very bad. Benek's shoulders shook but he could not yet speak.

"What is it, Benek? What has happened? Benek? Is it Cheshek?"

"No? News about father, then. Please tell me!" Jozef was beginning to panic, his mind was racing and screaming silently.

"No, it's not Cheshek or Tata." He managed to say in a whisper: "Mama is dead." A silence fell that seemed to stop time.

The brothers sat side-by-side staring at the floor in silence, watching their tears splash down and the droplets grow into a single pool.

Quietly, unwilling to accept it, Jozef murmured, "How do you know this? Who told you? Are you sure?" As he spoke, Jozef knew it was true. Their Mama was dead. After all they had endured, she was dead. Nothing in their lives would ever pain them as much as this.

The brothers stood and managed to walk outside, supporting each other but unable to speak. Their thoughts were with their beloved mother, who had nearly starved and worked herself to death to feed them, who went without to give her last mouthful of stale bread to Pola and Gina. For the rest of their lives none of them would ever forget the day that Mama had cooked and fed them grass to try and keep them alive.

When they looked back, they saw that they should have recognised her weakness. She never fully recovered after the loss of Mietek. She could barely manage to walk some days in the camp, when she was frozen and exhausted. Her hands would be bleeding from deep cracks in her skin; the hands that had been so elegant, with slender, nimble fingers, so diligent yet so calming. Even in her own lowest moments, she would still stroke a head in comfort and smile a loving smile.

The medical unit was near the sea and the sun began to tuck itself into the horizon. Half of the sky was ablaze with bright orange rays, mirrored in a sea of molten gold; an unreal vision in this land of unfamiliar sights and smells. The strangeness of this night would stay with the brothers always, the night when their lives would change forever.

As the sun disappeared completely and light faded further, the two brothers slowly walked along the sand. They came to a halt when they realised their feet were wet. Their night blindness was still playing tricks on them and they had walked into the sea.

They walked back to the hospital and received a hot drink of lemon tea. Only then was Benek able to explain that he had met up with Janina and in her own heartbreak, she had told him about Mama. She had met up with Lidia Czyz. Mrs Czyz, Mama's friend, told Janina that they had been on the boat together. She told Janina that Stasha had been feeling very tired and was going to find somewhere to lie down. She said that Stasha had seemed quiet and peaceful and was looking forward to being reunited with Pola and Gina. Mrs Czyz managed to sit down where she was and fell asleep.

The following morning, she awoke and looked for her friend. Lidia could not find her anywhere. She said that she managed to struggle through the crowds to the other side of the ship but it was difficult as there were so many people, many of whom were ill and lying on deck. She said that Stasha was nowhere to be found.

She saw a familiar face, a woman who had worked in the laundry and who they had seen when they boarded the ship. Lidia asked her if anyone had seen Mama, but no one had. Mrs Czyz then rounded the stern and saw a small gap in a crowd of people huddled on the deck.

With a great shock, she realised the group of men were throwing bodies into the sea. As she stood there, she saw them pick up Stasha's body and throw it overboard. Stasha had passed away during the night. They told her that so many people were dying that there was nothing else to do but commit their bodies to the sea.

Lidia Czyz had told Janina what a wonderful friend her Mama had been and that her life would now be empty without her. Lidia had put her arms around Janina and said she would never have been able to walk out of Russia if mamma had not given her the green shoes, which she was still wearing.

Starvation is an evil condition. A body can be wracked with hunger, yet it suffers and pains to survive. Then, when that body receives sustenance, food can often be the killer.

Once Stasha had felt hope for her children, the warmth

of sun on her face, felt reassurance that food would not be scarce, she was caught unawares. She stopped fighting for life and when her guard was down, it was taken from her.

Many decades later in her new life in America, and just before she herself passed away, Lidia Czyz still fondly remembered her close friend Stasha.

She related the story of the green shoes and recalled very clearly Janina's terrible sadness and her shock when she heard of the fate of her mother, unceremoniously tipped into foreign waters off an old rusting ship.

She said that she would be eternally grateful to God for a life touched by such friendship. Knowing Stasha had been a great privilege and her memory had always remained in her heart.

15. ELLAND, WEST YORKSHIRE

1955

"Your dad talks funny and you have a funny name."

"They say her dad's a German."

"My dad says my Uncle Malcolm was killed in the war by a German. It might have been her dad who shot my Uncle Malcolm."

"They say her dad shot Michael's Uncle Malcolm in the war!"

"My mum says I haven't to play with that Wizdank lass."

My name is Christine Marilyn Gwizdak. I am five years old and I live in Elland, in West Yorkshire. My mum is Doreen and my dad is Jozef. I have a brother called Richard who is six.

When you are five years old, you do not know a lot about different nationalities or geography, and I certainly don't know anything about this thing called "The War".

I live in a world where Mr. Blenkin, our ice-cream man, comes in a horse-drawn cart and rings his bell, and my friend Dane is the only person I know who has been abroad. He went on holiday to Jersey in a small plane. I know because he stood in front of the class and told us all about it.

We live in two adjoining houses, number 8 Eastgate and number 8a. One of the cottages used to be my Grandma Robinson's shop and the other is a small one-up, one-down. This had probably originally been occupied by a coach driver, as adjoining this dwelling is an old coach house, stables and hayloft. We have a large, cobbled back yard and through a gate, there is a big field.

Our home is not some sort of clever conversion. Two doors have been created between the two storeys of the houses and makeshift wooden steps are placed where the different floor levels do not match.

I cannot understand why my family is different from other people's families. When I ask a school friend to come to my house, she says, "I'm not allowed, my mum says you're not like us." Other people say such things as, "My nan says you should go back to where you came from!"

"What, me?" I ask. "I come from Elland. My mum says I was born in our house, number 8 Eastgate. I am where I come from."

To add to my confusion, I am called Marilyn by my family, although my first name is Christine. Grown-ups and teachers are not happy with my surname either, as they do not seem sure how to say it.

I start school, not a genius but not stupid either, to be confronted with "Christine Griezdal, are you deaf?" I am in trouble straightaway when I don't answer immediately, and then they say that I don't even know my own name! By the time I try to get through to them that, "I am called Marilyn and my last name is Gwizdak" I am already being led half way to the corner where I must stand still until told, with my nose against the wall until, they say, "You have remembered who you are."

Perhaps I was tinged with a slight eccentricity even then. I did not realise that everyone did not think in the same way I did, something that stays with me even today (later on in life, my husband Ed would affectionately say that I was "wired-up differently").

I am mystified. Some people are quite wonderful towards me but others can be really cruel. This is confusing and results in my analysing things too much. I dwell on things a lot and I decide that I am like an oyster: you either think I am delicious or you turn up your nose in disgust. There are no half measures where I am concerned.

I learn that I am half-Polish. Some of my best memories as a child are of the Polish Ex-Servicemen's Club in Halifax. I am told that many of the men, as with my own father, had been unable to return to Poland after something called The War. So dad stayed here and married our mum.

Some of Dad's fellow countrymen play the accordion at the Club on Saturday afternoons and it is here that my dad teaches me to dance to the Bluebell Polka. I am spellbound and find it all so very exciting. Mum tells Dad off when he lets Richard and me have a taste of something called Wisniowka. We also have delicious food that some people have never heard of.

Aunt Gina and Uncle Benny (Benek) and our cousins live locally and we are always welcome in their homes. Aunt Gina always makes delicious Polish food.

I have an Aunt Janina who lives in South America. She writes to us, but I have never seen her. Aunt Pola and Uncle Chester (Cheshek) live in London. When they come to visit us, they bring presents.

Uncle Chester has a poorly leg and when he came to visit us at Easter he brought some very special Easter eggs for us. They were imported from Czechoslovakia and had windows with pictures inside them.

Aunt Pola had a baby boy but he died. Afterwards, she had another son. I was pleased to hear that but I was still sad for her as I knew that one little person could not replace another.

I once asked my Dad where his parents were and he told

me that they were lost and missing in a land far away. My Dad would be sad and Grandma Robinson would say "Don't worry, Jozef, you've got me as your Mam now." Sometimes my dad looked upset and mum would say "Jozef, you must try and forget what happened to you all in Siberia." I did not know what this meant. I asked but they would not tell me.

Dad kept lots of chickens and we would sell our surplus eggs to our neighbours. I can still see him now, sitting on a stool in our cobbled backyard, wearing a black beret and whistling Doris Day's "Que Sera, Sera", plucking a chicken he had just killed, dipping it in a bucket of hot water, making it easier to pluck.

We had to grow up very quickly as regards our livestock. At first, some of the chickens were our pets. Then the realisation hit one day when we learned that our Sunday dinner had once had a name. Richard and I were upset, but dad told us not to be silly. He said that we didn't know what it was like to be hungry and have nothing to eat and that he would make sure that we never did. We never had lots of money, but we always had the best food. Mum cooked wonderful meals. However, I was still quite young when it dawned on me that hens and sheep were the same as roast chicken and lamb casserole.

Andrea, our sister, the baby of the family (called "Our Kid" until she was about thirty) was born when I was six. She missed out on playing a lot with Richard and me, being the youngest, but then again perhaps she was spared. I do recall that she was initiated into our world at about age two, when she was encouraged by us to witness the exhumation of our dead goldfish, who had been buried with full funereal honours a few weeks before.

This was important because we needed to see what he now looked like. However, the foil that mum had given us to use as Wilfred's shroud just looked disappointingly sludgy and nearly empty. I suppose we thought we would find a perfect fish skeleton that we could use to chase each other around the yard with.

It was a sad day for us all when Aunt Gina and her family left for a new life in California. Uncle Chester and his family had settled there and Aunts Janina and Pola were also now living in the USA. Our family and Uncle Benny's would not be emigrating, as our mums had parents and family here in the UK.

When I was about ten years old, Asian and West Indian people started arriving in our area. I felt sad because of the treatment they received from some, fortunately only a minority. I knew how they felt and that all this was just because they were a bit different. Nevertheless, I was still only a child and in my own young selfishness, I knew they now had someone else to pick on and might leave the Polish people alone. Well, some did anyway.

1980s

Visits between America and Great Britain have become more frequent and now we are getting to know Dad's relatives more closely. Aunt Janina, Dad's sister, and her son, Andrzej ("Andrew" or "Kuba" to his family) are planning a trip to Poland. They will visit the old village in Poland where the Gwizdak family grew up, somewhere called Puzieniewicze and they are going to make a video of their trip. They will also meet up with some of our more distant relatives during their stay.

Aunt Janina will also visit Irena Krol, her life-long friend from her school days in Poland. Irena lives in London. This is all very interesting to me. I want to know more.

On one of these exchanges, Aunt Janina brought a gift for my Dad and Uncle Benny. She has kept this photograph for over fifty years. Her brothers were unaware that it existed and have not seen it since they were children.

This was the picture that Janina took from their home

when they were evicted and transported to Siberia. She hid it in her clothing, risking punishment as personal possessions were not allowed, and kept it all these years without showing it to them. Although badly damaged, she had two copies enlarged and framed and she presented these to her brothers. I was not there to witness this but I am told that when they received them, it was an extremely emotional moment.

The photograph is of their mother and father, sitting outside their house in Puzieniewicze with dad's brother, Uncle Frank, who helped their father to build the house. They had not seen a picture of their parents for over fifty years. I look at the photograph and realise that this is the family and the grandparents that I never knew and I want to hear more about them.

1995

I am now in my mid-forties, married to Edward. We have a daughter Alexandra, our only child, who is at university in London. These days I have a little more time to think and reflect. I turn my interest to my family background and I begin to ask more and more questions.

I persuade my dad, who is now in his late seventies, to talk about his life before he came to Britain, something he has never wished to do before. I tell him that I want to write it all down. Initially, he just says "Marilyn, who will be interested? No one will want to know. You waste your time."

It soon meant something to me to hear about Dad being a soldier in the First Polish Paratrooper Brigade and being dropped over Arnhem and wounded at the battle for Driel.

This is where our story begins to take hold of me and I cannot stop thinking about it. I read as much as I can about the subject and discover a lot about World War II. Not much is written about the unbelievable plight of the Polish people at that time; about the labour camps in Siberia and the story of their incredible journey.

I hear from Dad, for the first time, the very sad story of my grandmother and how she lost her life. I realise that she was younger when she died than I was at the time of hearing about it.

I learn that the Dutch Government still treats my father and his comrades as heroes and invites them as guests to yearly remembrance ceremonies. I also know that the Polish Ex-Servicemen were not invited to march in the Victory Parade in London.

Something is slightly amiss and I need to know what it is all about. So over the next ten years I talk to my father, Jozef, at great length, and my Uncles Benny and Chester, about their lives before they left Eastern Europe. I visit my relatives in the USA and talk to them. Although they were very young, they recall some very poignant moments. Although, one thing is clear, I have to be so careful and sensitive as any questioning about their childhood, Poland and Siberia, proves profoundly painful to them all.

I visit Poland several times and decide to do some of my own research. I discovered so much but one question still remained unanswered: what happened to our grandfather?

My father was in occupied Germany for a few years after the war so was unable at the time to make any enquiries about his father. As soon as they were able, Janina and the rest of the family contacted the Red Cross, who had had many enquiries from other families but there was still no trace of any of the husbands and fathers who were arrested and taken away in 1939.

They began to ask as many people and organisations as they could if there was any news of the Polish officers who had just seemed to disappear. This was not just a handful of men but more than twenty thousand.

The Gwizdak family had already heard, near the end of the war, of the discovery of a dreadful tragedy connected to the disappearance of 4,421 Polish officers and officials. This was to become known as The Katyn Massacre. It is now known that this discovery came about when the German army invaded Russia in the spring of 1943.

An international commission of twelve medical experts visited Katyn in 1943 at the invitation of the Germans. Investigators and forensic experts were sent to the site and the area was fully excavated and the bodies exhumed while the war was still going on. However, many of the details of the search were not revealed to the public at that time.

There was a lot of propaganda created regarding this incident. The Germans claimed that the Russians had carried out the killings and the Russians denied this and blamed the massacre on the Germans.

It is written that, after the War during the Nuremberg Trials, a Colonel Ahrens testified that a wolf had dug holes in the ground and retrieved bones. This took place in a forest in Russia near Katyn. It was discovered that the bones were human and this was the site of a mass grave. The feral dogs had found the killing fields of thousands of Polish officers. These men had their hands tied behind their backs with wire and had been shot through the back of their heads. Some had sawdust stuffed in their mouths, probably to quieten them. They had been unceremoniously dumped in pits that had been dug in advance.

Every one of the bodies was exhumed and identified and the shocking body count was revealed. The dead numbered: 1 admiral, 2 generals, 24 colonels, 79 lieutenant colonels, 258 majors, 654 captains, 17 naval captains, 3,420 NCOs, 7 chaplains, 3 landowners, 1 prince, 43 officials, 85 privates, 131 refugees, 20 university professors, 300 physicians, several hundred lawyers, engineers, teachers, more than 100 writers and journalists and 200 pilots.

A number of denominations were represented: Orthodox and Catholic Christians, Protestants, Jews and Muslims.

Details of this massacre were only sparsely available. Little was known or written about for nearly fifty years. To mention this massacre in Poland following the war, during

Soviet occupation, meant the loss of one's employment or home or attracted further punishment. This warned an already oppressed nation of further retribution should anyone pursue the subject. A whole generation of Polish nationals had grown up denied the full history of their people. Fortunately, there have been many families and societies throughout the world that have kept this piece of history alive within their own communities.

The one thing that we did know for over forty years was that Andrzej Gwizdak, our grandfather, was not found and exhumed in the Katyn Forest.

So what happened to him and a further 16,000 or more Polish Officers?

16. STOLPSE RAILWAY STATION, NOWOGRODEK, POLAND, 1939

After saying goodbye to Stasha and the children, Andrzej and twenty-three of his fellow military settlers, friends and neighbours from Puzieniewicze were rounded up and marched at gunpoint to the police station in Turzec a few kilometres away. They were locked up in adjoining buildings, where they were held for two days.

Jozef arrived in Turzec and went straight to the police station where his father was being held. He brought tobacco, a food parcel and a few personal items. At first, he was told that he could not see his father, but Jozef persisted and made a nuisance of himself. Finally, they relented. He was led to another part of the building and managed to see his father, although only through a window.

"Tata, I will talk to them again and ask them what is going on. They have no right to keep you locked up here. I thought it was Germany who we were supposed to be at war with? I will come back again tomorrow. See you then. Bye Tata."

"Goodbye, Jozef. Look after your mother and your brothers and sisters."

Jozef felt troubled by the seemingly resigned attitude of his father. Driven by his youthful sense that the world would bend to his will, if only he pushed hard enough, he had yet to appreciate that his father's assessment of the situation was calculated from many years of experience.

Jozef left with a sense of frustration and foreboding. He walked across the yard to the corner of the building and before he stepped out of sight, he turned, catching a final glimpse of his father. Their hands raised, their eyes locked, father and son nodded and waved.

On turning the corner of the building, Jozef ran into Katya, the Russian girl he had danced with. This was the first time he had met her since that night. He told her how sorry he was that his father had acted the way he had. She was very sweet and said she knew that it was nothing personal. She said she understood why he would do that. They said their goodbyes.

When Jozef returned to Turzec the following day, the building was empty. Andrzej and the other men had gone.

Earlier that day, Andrzej and his fellow prisoners had been woken before first light.

"Get up! Get your things together. We are leaving in ten minutes."

"Where are we going?"

"Is it true that we are being taken to fight alongside the Russians?"

"No more questions! You must follow orders!"

The atmosphere was threatening and the men knew that this was to be a less than friendly and co-operative operation. Russian guards appeared at the door and pointed at the exit with the muzzles of their guns. The men were led out into the yard.

A heavily pockmarked man with no neck stood before them. He spoke in Russian. His adjutant, a skinny, weak-looking man, echoed a translation in very poor Polish. "You will join troop train at Stolpse station. We ask no trouble. Remember family. If you give trouble, they will get trouble.

Understand, yes?"

The men were led out. The heavens opened and torrential rain turned the streets into rivers. They marched for hours. The men were hungry, wet and cold.

Blat-blat sounds were heard in the distance: stifled gunfire. They left the road and took a short cut across fields. The mud was thick, their boots sank deep. There was a smell of burning wood. Andrzej had a nauseous feeling of deja vu. They arrived at a road outside the station.

They were held there for a while and surprisingly, while they were waiting, they were encouraged to write a message to their families, letting them know that all was well. They arrived at the station. Cattle trucks were awaiting their next consignment of passengers.

"Get in the trucks!"

"Where are we going?"

"Silence! No more questions!"

There was a tangible edginess amongst the Russian troops. This was understandable as all the men under guard were well-trained ex-Polish Army officers or other equally high-raking officials.

Half of the men had climbed onto the train when a Russian officer appeared. He spoke in educated Polish. "You are to be taken to an undisclosed place in Russia, to a prison camp."

Some of the men, despite the threats, tried to protest. "We are not at war with Russia; why are we prisoners?"

For a moment, the officer appeared to listen and take their questions seriously. They presented the logical argument that if they were allowed to go back to their lands, they could support their families and provide much needed food for a Europe at war.

But then he said, "You are Poland's staunchest defenders, ex-soldiers, fighting men. Can we trust you? I am Mother Russia's staunchest defender. Would I ever compromise my allegiance? No! Well?"

There was no response.

"There is your answer!"

After a minute, someone made a stand. "Russia has not declared war on Poland and therefore our status as prisoners of war should be negated."

With that, and a nod from the officer, a rifle butt struck the head of one of the prisoners and blood began to trickle down his face.

"Let that be a lesson to you all! No more questions and no more trouble."

Meanwhile, hundreds more men were arriving at the station on foot each hour, while trucks loaded with further prisoners were arriving by the dozen.

Andrzej and his comrades huddled together and whispered between themselves. "What the hell is going on? It looks like the entire police force from all over the region has been rounded up." And so it had.

A further consignment arrived: officials, administrators, even boy-scout leaders. All protests were futile and the men felt increasingly threatened. As the masses grew, it was apparent that the group could get out of control and the Russian guards were beginning to get very edgy. They quickened their pace.

Orders were shouted: "Get in the trucks now! Any retaliation and remember your families are vulnerable. Need we say more?"

Andrzej and his neighbours were herded in together. The trains were packed with as many men as each truck could hold and the doors were immediately bolted.

A shot rang out, this time in close proximity. Their silence was assured by the threat. They sat and waited in the cattle trucks for the rest of the day and all of the night as more men were loaded onto the waiting transport. They had not eaten for forty-eight hours, they had nothing to drink and the temperature was now well below zero.

So began the exodus of the first convoy of hundreds of

thousands of men from all parts of Eastern Poland to camps in the Soviet Union.

The journey took many days and nights, as ever, due to the Russian troop convoys taking precedence. From day one, the least important issue regarding their evacuation and transportation was reasonable food and water. Within a few weeks, and throughout October, the men were barely managing on meagre rations and many were falling ill.

1939 saw one of the coldest winters on record in Eastern Europe and as the convoy reached its destination, a lake between Moscow and Leningrad (St Petersburg), many men had already succumbed to hypothermia and frostbite.

There were no adequate medical provisions and the bitter cold was unrelenting. Many more trucks arrived in the area daily and within weeks the interned men, in this one camp alone, totalled nearly 7,000.

The men were forced into hard labour on a huge lumber project. Those with frostbite in their fingers and toes were not exempted from work and even the strongest among them began to feel the strain.

Andrzej sat in a dark corner of a high-vaulted chapel, huddled in a group that consisted of some of the men from back home. Their mumbled words, made more obvious at a distance by the vapour of their breath, echoed and dispersed into the void. One by one, they stood to stretch their cold-cramped legs; their hands, wrapped tightly around their chests, occasionally moved to slap their sides in an attempt to improve circulation.

Antoni Swiercz, the former district administrator back home in Puzieniewicze and, like Andrzej, a veteran of two wars, said a few words. They tried to stay positive although they were uncomfortably aware they were being watched.

The draughts whistled down the main aisles of the austere galleries. Any barrier against the unrelenting cold was welcomed. Wood fires burned and the smoke lingered.

"My prison is a monastery situated on Stolbnyi Island in the middle of Lake Seliger, Russia. Accessed only by a long bridge, it is situation on an island in what is said to be one of the purest lakes in all Eastern Europe. I suppose that in another world, or at another time this area would be regarded as a place of beauty; but not this particular winter……"

It was two weeks before Christmas 1939. During the winter months, in an attempt to keep mind, body and soul together, the men tried to keep occupied whenever they had spare time. When the temperature was below minus forty degrees, they were unable to do any work. No one could survive these temperatures for more than half an hour. At such times, when they were holed up in the freezing halls, they found pastimes to sustain themselves.

They had managed to stack piles of off-cuts of wood that were no longer needed and they set about creating bunk-beds. Anything was preferable to sleeping on the cold floors.

When this was complete, many men continued to work with wood.

"Who taught you to carve wood, Stefan?"

"My grandfather. The old chap used to supplement the family's income when he got older. When the rheumatism in his legs became too much for him to work alongside my father, this is what he did. Decorative plates were his specialty. He and grandmother would sell them at the local market. My father was never all that good at it but they said I had the flair."

"I'd like to have a go. Will you teach me?"

"Yeah, sure."

Woodcarving had become one of the many shared activities, with one man teaching another the rudiments of the craft. Many of the men started to make wooden pallets to wear on their feet attached with leather straps. Nothing was thrown away and they all learned to be thrifty and make something out of any old scrap.

To add to their misery, many of the men began to fall ill with tuberculosis and there were more and more cases as the weeks passed by.

"Tadek, I hear that Zygmunt died during the night. I am sorry. God be with you."

"Dziekuje, Krzystof. He has been coughing up blood for weeks now and he just got weaker and weaker. I could only sit by and watch him suffer. He is at peace now; his suffering is over."

"As cousins, he and I were brought up together. His mother died when his younger brother was born. He lived with us also, but he was handicapped and died when he was only little."

Tadek's mind was going over his time as a boy. Happy times, playing with Zygmunt on the farm and growing up together; the kind of thoughts often only provoked by the finality of death and the sudden reminder of one's own mortality.

"Can I swap something for his belt?" said Kryzstof, feeling embarrassed to ask when the man had only been dead a few hours. Tadek nodded and Krystof gave him a handkerchief to cover Zygmunt's face. That way a blanket was not wasted on a dead man when everyone was suffering from the cold.

"What do you want it for? I see that you already have a belt."

"I am going to strip it down into thongs and patches. I have seen some of the other men doing this. They use it to repair their boots. Some of the men are also making sandals to wear at night, so they don't spend all their time with wet feet."

The men helped each other out as much as possible. There was an assurance and understanding here, for no one knew how long it would be before they too might need someone's help. Before long, their own fingers could be rendered useless due to frostbite. Then they could hope that help would be reciprocated. Many men had now completely lost use of their hands. Blackened fingers and toes were a common sight.

Some had only been wearing a jacket when they were arrested and not many of them had been able to bring an overcoat. Also, in this weather, boot leather easily cracked. They were not suitably attired for the extreme climate.

The old monastery buildings offered no comfort to a man freezing with a sodden wool uniform and no change of clothes. Times were sad when men sat waiting for another's last breath and then waited just a little longer, out of respect, before they dared to remove an item that could help to keep someone else alive for another day.

Chess and other gaming pieces were carved to break the monotony of their imprisonment. Some of the men worked on little trinket boxes, in hopes of being reunited with a daughter, girlfriend, wife or mother.

However basic and shabby their surroundings were, the men upheld standards that showed their self-discipline. They were men who had been accustomed to immaculate grooming, a habit probably ingrained in them from military training.

Two men broke the layer of ice on a bowl of water. "This razor has had it now. I find it very irritating not to be able to shave properly."

"We are now exhausting our supply. Of all the hundreds of men who have already gone, there was not a decent razor to be had among them."

"Here, sharpen this." Another of their comrades handed over a cut-throat razor. "You will have to get used to using this from now on if you don't want to grow a beard."

"Maybe I will give the beard a try. Perhaps it will keep my face warmer."

However squalid their surroundings, the men managed to wash and re-use the cotton handkerchiefs they had on their person when they were arrested. Handkerchiefs are nearly always given as a gift by womenfolk and many of these had hand-embroidered monograms. These would no doubt be a comforting possession to have in such a dreadful place.

Among their only other possessions were crucifixes, prayer books, lighters and watches.

Andrzej saw that his neighbour was holding a photograph that he had taken out of his pocket. "I never had the opportunity; we were marched away so quickly. It never occurred to me that we would not see our families for all this time." Andrzej tried to picture the faces of Stasha and his children and felt panic when he did not seem to have instant recall. He was missing his tobacco and felt that he'd be much calmer if he had some.

It was apparent that the inmates of this huge camp comprising thousands of men would provide an elite fighting force if called upon to defend their country. The entire police force from North Eastern Poland had been forcibly disbanded and many of them had been transported to this labour camp. Along with Andrzej and his fellow high-ranking army veterans and landowners were priests, officials, community leaders, border guards and anyone who was highly educated or who may have been considered a political dissident or threat.

Christmas 1939 was filled with thoughts of family and loved ones. Although the men could not celebrate with feasting and gifts, it was a more profoundly religious festival than most had experienced in past years. They prayed hard and long and then prayed again for their prayers to be heard. They had only one wish.

The men had been allowed to write to their families twice since they were captured. But more recently, they had been denied communication with the outside world.

The days came and went without any change and no news of the war in Europe. There were few visitors to the camp. Any such people, like drivers collecting the logs, were under strict instruction not to talk to the inmates.

Again and again, Andrzej and the men were called for further interrogations. Over and over, the same questions were asked.

"What did they ask you, Andrzej?" whispered Antoni, avoiding detection by known spies in the camp.

"The same questions as ever," was the reply.

"Same here."

"I've heard that if you don't give them the answers they want, you'll be sentenced to hard labour in one of the toughest arctic gulags," said a heavy-set ex-policeman.

"We don't know that to be true. The situation here is not good anyway, so we don't need speculation of that kind," said Antoni Swiecz.

"Speculation? I hope so, but the guards were overheard saying that ten years in a camp in Kamchatka is on the cards. The higher your rank, the heavier your sentence."

"Looks like we will get the same sentence then, Andrzej," said Antoni with spirit.

"We are our own worse enemies in this situation but I will not compromise," said Andrzej.

"We are the same, my friend", said Antoni.

The weather lightened and at last the men felt a thaw was beginning. After a few more weeks, news began to circulate that some of them were to be released. "We have heard from a driver of rumours that we are to be released and reunited with our families."

Sure enough, shortly afterwards a small group of men were released. Following this there were no further releases but at the beginning of May, the men were told that they would be transported out of the camp to another location.

Russian soldiers and officials, reputed to be members of the NKVD, arrived in the camp.

"You will be relocated in small groups. Your name and identity number will be called out as the transport arrives.

You are to move quickly. You will be taken to a collection area for further transport to be arranged. The quicker we can turn around the trucks, the quicker you will all be out of here."

"Andrzej, it is obvious that they need us to fight."

"The Germans must be closing in, so they are desperate!"

He turned to his friend and comrade, "Antoni, I don't know which is the lesser of two evils. If we had the choice, would we stay here or fight in the Russian Army?"

"It is as well that the choice is not ours."

"The state most of us are in, we are not fit for a fighting force."

"This is Russia, remember. Ninety-nine per cent of their army have never had a decent meal in their lives."

"What troubles me is that all this is taking so long, only about 250 men per night. Then the trucks are back the next day."

"Where do you think they are taking us?"

"I'd say that with the 6,000 or more men now left in this camp, they must be transporting just a few per day, probably to the nearest train station and integrating us into Russian troop convoys."

Over the next couple of months through April and May, vehicles arrived to transport the men away. The monastery was slowly being cleared.

Andrzej's call came to evacuate. A surly, adipose man with a square face read out the day's list.

"Andrzej Gwizdak, year of birth 1897, son of Jakuba Gwizdak, identity no: 7316." Andrzej noted that he was number ten on this list.

The system of selection and order did not seem to follow any pattern. The group of 250 men were marched to waiting trucks.

Many thought that there could be no worse place than where they had spent the last the eight months. A large number of men had perished that winter. It was sad to think they had died and their families knew nothing.

The men travelled mainly in silence, just waiting and wondering about their destination. Any enquiries about where they were to be taken were met with answers such as "no information, secret troop movement".

The trucks stopped at the railway station of Soroga, where the men were herded under armed guard onto prison rail cars. The route went via Likhoslavi onto Kalinin.

Prison buses collected the men at the station and transported them to the District Board of the NKVD and a prison situated on Sovetskaya Street.

It was already dark when the buses eventually came to a standstill. They were parked for some considerable time. It appeared, for what they could gather, that all the buses were lined up just waiting. The men could only guess that the Russians were trying to stagger the integration of so many men onto further transport.

The occupants were ordered to alight, a bus at a time, and were ushered into a courtyard and told to wait. Then they were led into cells in the basement of the Prison where, again, they would wait.

They were told that they were to be questioned further and would receive instructions before being assigned to transport groups for relocation.

There was an air of uncertainty.

"What questions? I have nothing more to say," said a middle-aged Police Chief.

"They seem to be going to a lot of trouble though," said a colleague.

The group was then split into smaller groups still and at staggered intervals led out of the cells into another building.

"What the hell is that noise?" asked one of the men.

"Some sort of generator, perhaps?"

"It's very loud."

"Silence!" an NKVD officer barked. They were hurried

along a corridor.

"Wait here. You will be taken in one at a time. Your details will be checked and you will receive further travel documents."

"Number 1897, Andrzej Gwizdak: follow me!"

"Down these stairs to the office." Andrzej was led into a basement room where a handful of Russian officers stood.

Two guards arrived, checked his identity and marched him along a corridor into a side room. The room was painted red. Andrzej could smell the alcohol on them straight away: these men were drunk. Panic suddenly seized him. "What the hell is going on?"

The noise was deafening. Andrzej decided it was some kind of engine-driven machinery. It was disconcerting as the noise was so loud, it was hard to think straight, let alone hear anything around him.

The guards at either side of him roughly pulled his hands behind his back and tied his wrists with wire. Panic set in.

He was restrained and dragged into a further room. This had been crudely soundproofed with what looked like velvet on the walls.

No one spoke. He saw a red-faced, stocky Russian, wearing a leather apron and gloves. As he attempted to speak, something was roughly stuffed into his mouth.

Andrzej was forced to his knees. Is he to be tortured? What for? What does he know?

A shot rang out. Andrzej Gwizdak fell. He had been killed instantly with a gunshot to the back of his head.

The man with the leather apron reloaded his gun as two men grabbed Andrzej's feet and dragged him out leaving a large blood trail. Another man hosed down the sloping floor and the water ran into a drain hole in one corner.

The next man was brought in and the process was repeated again and again.

Andrzej's body, along with that evening's consignment of murdered men, Poland's most loyal and patriotic defenders, were loaded onto trucks and driven thirty-two kilometres along the Moscow to Leningrad Road. The flat-bed trucks arrived in the town of Miednoye on the Tversa River and then continued onto a forest clearing.

There he was randomly dumped in an open pit four to six metres deep along with 249 of his murdered fellow countrymen. For nearly a month, an excavator would cover the pits with earth and dig another one on a daily basis.

This would be the mass-grave and final resting place of nearly 7,000 men: a forest hidden deep on Russian soil. The whereabouts of these husbands, fathers, sons and brothers would be unknown to the world for over fifty years.

17. EPILOGUE

It is as well that our grandmother did not know of our grandfather's fate before she died. I cannot imagine that she would have possessed the strength to keep her family together as she did in Siberia, had she known the truth. I am sure that her dreams of the family being reunited kept her going during her darkest hours.

The reality was that Andrzej had already been murdered when Stasha and the children had been in the camp for only a few weeks.

It is at this juncture that I wish to express my utmost respect for her and acknowledge that, without my grandmother's courage and endurance, we would not be the family we are today. My gratitude goes out to a woman to whom we owe so much. I deeply regret that I never had the privilege of meeting and getting to know her.

The truth about my grandfather emerged during the mid-1990s when I acquired a copy of a newly-published book listing the names of the officers executed and buried in mass graves in three different locations in Russia.

Lists of names of the men exhumed at Katyn have been available for some time. The mass graves at Miednoye and Charkow, however, were only discovered, excavated and partly exhumed in the early to mid-1990s.

During my research, I was also given a copy of a death warrant, signed by Stalin, bearing my grandfather's name.

In the year 2000, monuments were installed and consecrated at the three known sites of mass graves. Austere, eight-metre-high crosses rise into the pine canopies. A semi-subterranean bell was chosen as the symbol marking each site. Resounding both above and below ground, it announces that what was hidden below ground for so long is now known and will not be forgotten.

I was even more inspired to write my story when I visited a museum outside Warsaw in 2006, now a memorial to all the men who were executed. I personally feel that the naming of the museum "Katyn" and referring to all of the executions as "The Katyn Massacre" is misleading and also rather disparaging. The collective losses should not share the name of only one of the sites of the mass graves. The Katyn forest, the site of over 4,000 graves, has been known about since 1943, although not widely publicised.

Miednoye and Charkow are much more recent discoveries and should be commemorated independently. After all, more than 16,000 further graves have been identified. Combining these massacres under the umbrella of Katyn will, I feel, only prevent people from truly grasping the scale of this tragedy.

Unlike Katyn, attempted exhumation of the two further sites proved to be practically impossible after over fifty years. Since the Russians buried the men's scant belongings and possessions in a separate pit that was fully excavated. The retrieved items are now on display at the Citadel in Warsaw.

I was proud to witness the new chapel in Warsaw's Military Cathedral, where the walls are lined with steel plaques bearing the name of every man known to have lost his life in these executions.

In autumn 2007, the Polish Government awarded posthumous promotions to all men whose remains were identified in the three burial areas. Their names were read out over the course of three days and two nights, continuously. Andrzej Gwizdak, my grandfather, was one of these men.

A thought must be spared for the remaining lost men, lying in unknown graves, hidden somewhere on Russian soil. It was decided that only the names of the men whose bodies were located could be honoured and named on the memorials, so there is a need for the Russian Government to be pressed for information disclosing the whereabouts of the missing, though further mass graves have now been unearthed and the total is now over 30,000 victims.

In October 2007, the Polish government declared April 13th 2008 to be a national holiday: Katyn Memorial Day. In April 2008, my father, Jozef Gwizdak, accompanied by my brother Richard, my mother Doreen and I, attended the first official commemoration service in Warsaw.

My father, Jozef Gwizdak, was 85 years old and this was to be his last visit to his homeland. It was his wish to say his own goodbye to the land of his birth and forefathers.

In Warsaw, we visited the Monument to the Evacuees. I found it to be a wonderful work of art, evoking an immediate, heartfelt response.

Finally, at a formal ceremony, standing beneath trees laden with mistletoe, my brother and I laid a wreath in the Military Cemetery in Warsaw in memory of our grandfather, Andrzej Gwizdak, and all those who perished alongside him.

A further visit to Warsaw: My husband Edward and I received an invitation to a private pre-opening viewing of the New Katyn Museum, just a short walk from the centre of the city.

Now housed in the imposing "Citadel", (built primarily as a prison by Tsar Nicholas 1 in 1831), it now houses the dedicated exhibition related to the Katyn massacres. The museum is impressive, poignant, harrowing but worthily commemorative.

Further memorial chapels have been built to commemorate the victims. Again, as with the Military Cathedral in Warsaw, a metal plaque bears the name of each victim. I sought out the name of my grandfather with pride.

Following our tour, we had a presentation by a Polish historian. It was here that I learned for the first time that the names and addresses of the families deported to Siberia were taken from the final censored communications sent by the arrested men, prior them being taken across the border into Russian and subsequent imprisonment and execution.

The addresses on the correspondence from the men to their families were used to locate and deport the family. This would be the reason why some families may have been spared – no letter, no deportation.

We were also very honoured to meet General Anders daughter, Anna Maria, at a ceremony at the "Monument to the Murdered and Fallen in the East".

This amazing bronze sculpture was created by the artist Maksymilian Biskupski in 1995 and we felt very privileged to share his company at dinner that same evening.

In a modern society, every atrocity warrants a memorial in history; we cannot move on without recognising our debt to those who gave their lives.

Now is the time to acknowledge the suffering of the Polish Nation during World War Two. It is owed recognition, respect and commemoration.

And this is the main purpose of my book.

18. HISTORY

Eye Witness Accounts of Executions

On the 6th October 1991, The Observer Newspaper printed an article based on eyewitness reports of the executions at Kalinin in the Basement of the NKVD Headquarters.

A retired NKVD Agent Vladimir Tokaryev, who in 1991 was 89, blind and living in a flat in the city of Vladimir, broke his 50 year silence and confessed on tape that he was witness to the executions.

He also implicated another agent, Pyotr Soprunenko, who in 1991 was 83 and living in an apartment in central Moscow. Although denying involvement and stating he could not remember, he was shown documents bearing his name.

A team of Soviet military prosecutors who were ordered by President Gorbachev to investigate the Soviet Union's role in the Katyn and other killings made the tape.

The Guardian newspaper holds a copy of this tape.

Stalin's Chief Executioner

During April and May 1940, when Germany and the Soviet Union were still best friends and digesting Poland's carcass, the Russians quietly, systematically and efficiently murdered an estimated 30,000+ mostly Polish Officers, policemen and intellectuals. Although the murders occurred in at least six locations through the Western Soviet Union, the Katyn Forest, where 4,4000 were killed, lent it name to all those executed as the Katyn Massacre. In the NKVD headquarters in Kalinin (now called Tver) northwest of Moscow, Vasili Mikhailovich Blokhin, Joseph Stalin's chief executioner, personally shot thousands of Polish Officers, over six thousand men.

In the 1920s Blokhin rose rapidly in the NKVD the People's Commissariat for Internal Affairs, otherwise known as the Soviet Secret Police. Stalin himself noted Blokhin's mastery of assassinations, torture and clandestine executions – "black work". Blokhin soon found himself in charge of a small special branch of the NKVD that specialised in "black work" answerable only to Stalin himself and was made a Major General. As the Soviet chief executioner, he went about his work without a paper trail and minimum scrutiny.

Blokhin's Assignment

In early 1940, Soviet leader Joseph Stalin decided he wanted to eliminate Polish nationalists and "counter-revolutionaries" in order to remove obstacles to his future plans for Poland. Based on the 4th April 1940 secret order from Stalin to Lavrenti Beria, the NKVD was tasked with eliminating 25,000 Polish "prisoners".

Vasili Blokhin was given the assignment to get rid of Polish officers held at the Ostashkow POW camp. (This "POW" status was rejected by Poland, as Russia had never declared war on Poland and therefore they were civilians not POW's.)

As was his custom, Blokhin carefully considered all the variables and made his plans. First the prisoners had to be transported from Ostashkow to Kalinin, a distance of over a hundred miles, so trucks, fuel, drivers and prison trains were allocated to ensure that each evening the Poles were delivered to Kalinin Prison. Blokhin calculated how many of his men would be needed to follow the execution procedures: getting the prisoners from the trucks into the prison, then escorting each one down to the execution chamber and removing each body to waiting flatbed trucks. Twice a night, the covered trucks would transport the murdered officers a short distance to freshly dug trenches, where bodies were thrown. He allocated one bulldozer and two NKVD drivers to fill the trenches.

At first he'd hoped to kill 300 prisoners a night, but then determined that this would put a strain on him and his men. He reckoned he could shoot a prisoner every 2-3 minutes continuously for roughly ten hours between sundown and dawn and so revised his plans based on killing 250 a night for 28 nights.

28 Nights of Shooting

Starting in April 1940, after the sun went down, the process started. A Polish officer was led to the "Leninist Room", painted red, where he was identified and handcuffed. Guards then restrained him and took him next door to the execution chamber. Its walls were padded, the floor sloped towards a drain; a hose was available. Waiting inside was Vasili Blokhin, decked out in a leather butcher's apron, leather hat and large leather gloves. Without comment or formality, Blokhin put his pistol at the base of the prisoner's skull and shot him once with a German Walther Model 2.25 ACP pistol. He had a briefcase full of his own pistols, since he did not trust the reliability of the standard-issue Soviet TT-30 for the frequent heavy-use he intended. Blokhin's men then removed the body through another door to the waiting trucks. Then the process restarted with the next prisoner and the next, until the night's quota of 250 Poles were all dead and gone. With the night's work done, Blokhin provided vodka for all his men. An estimated 30 NKVD men were needed to carry out his orders.

It was revealed in records many years later that the men attending these executions were seriously affected by the scale of the slaughter and were given large amounts of vodka to enable them to carry on.

Blokhin's Career and Fall

Blokhin was awarded the Order of the Badge of Honour (1937), the Order of the Red Banner (1941) and a monthly bonus from Stalin for "his skill and organisation in the effective carrying-out of special tasks". During his career, Blokhin is said to have personally killed, before, during and after the war, tens of thousands, including Soviet officials who fell out of favour. His was the finger on the trigger for every high official Stalin executed during the Great Purge of the Thirties, the highest being Marshall of the Soviet Union, Mikhail Tukhachevsy in 1937.

After Stalin died in 1953, Vasili Blokhin was forcibly retired and stripped of his rank. According to Soviet records, he sank in alcoholism, went insane and committed suicide on February 3rd 1955 at the age of 60. (Author's Note: Readers can be forgiven for believing that Blokhin was insane all along).

Hitler's Solution

For five years, Poland endured the most severe wartime occupation conditions in modern European history. Germany annexed western Poland directly, establishing a brutal, colonial government whose expressed goal was to erase completely the concept of Polish nationhood and make Poles the slaves of a new German empire.

About one million Poles were removed from German-occupied areas and replaced with German settlers. An additional 2.5 million Poles went into forced labour camps in Germany.

The statement of Adolf Hitler to his Army commanders on 22nd August 1939, reads:

"Thus for the time being I have sent to the East only my 'Death's Head Units' with the orders to kill without pity or mercy all men, women, children of Polish race or language. Only in such a way will we win the vital space that we need. Who still talks nowadays about the Armenians?"

Stalin's Solution

In September 1939, it is estimated that the Soviets detained 250,000 purported prisoners-of-war from eastern Poland. The NKVD segregated what they regarded as the intelligentsia (the educated classes).

An estimation of up to 25,000+ Polish officers was executed at the command of secret police-chief Lavrenty Beria, on Stalin's orders.

Over 14,000 were discovered in mass graves in three locations …

- Katyn: 4,421 (discovered and exhumed in 1943)
- Charkow: 3,820 (discovered and partially exhumed in the mid-1990s)
- Miednoye: 6,311 (discovered and partially exhumed in the mid-1990s).

The remainder, it is reported, were detained in one hundred transition camps in the eastern third of the USSR.

By the year 2005, more than 10,000 men were still missing, their location unknown.

Despite Soviet aggression on 17th September 1939, the Poles never declared war on the USSR. Therefore, the murdered Poles did not have proper POW status. They were civilians.

The Russians did not execute a defeated enemy but systematically eliminated any Polish citizen who could potentially oppose them, much like the Khmer Rouge did in Cambodia.

In all, the NKVD eliminated almost half of the Polish Officer Corps as part of Stalin's long-term effort to prevent the resurgence of an independent Poland.

Post-war, in 1945, a Soviet court tried ten officers of the German Wehrmacht for involvement in the massacre of the 4,421 men at Katyn. Seven were hanged on the same day that their trial concluded for a crime their prosecutors knew they had not committed.

Soviet authorities refused to admit responsibility until nearly the end of the Union in 1991. Poland regards the massacres as the ultimate symbol of Soviet cruelty and mendacity. Pressured to confess to the slaughter, Mikhail Gorbachev admitted that the killings had been perpetrated by Stalin's secret police. Boris Yeltsin handed over two-thirds of the documented evidence to Lech Walesa in 1991.

So it was, during the mid-1990s that many of us begin to discover the secrets of Miednoye and Charkow and the whereabouts of these mass graves, some sixty years later.

Sadly, at that time further records had been retained and the resting place of the remaining estimated 10,000 was still unknown.

The NKVD filmed the executions carried out in Smolensk. During the Korean War, it is reported that the Soviets gave North Korea a copy of the film for instructional purposes.

Big Three: allies and poor relations

After the discovery of the Katyn graves by German troops in 1943, Stalin claimed to be 'offended' by the Polish insistence on an independent investigation and broke off diplomatic relations with the exiled Polish government. Poland's future now lay in the hands of her Western allies.

The Soviets denied any responsibility for the politically explosive massacres at Katyn and insisted that the crimes had been committed in 1941, when the area was under German control. Churchill, while privately admitting his belief in Soviet culpability, assured the Soviets that no investigation would take place.

When Stalin was questioned about the whereabouts of the thousands more Polish officers who had disappeared, he replied that they had been dispersed to labour camps throughout the Soviet Union. The Allies knew the value of such an elite fighting force and called for their reinstatement. It was then reported that Stalin made one phone call. He asked if all his orders had been carried out. On affirmation, it was rumoured that he refused to speak to anyone.

This was a delicate matter for the Allies; overnight, Stalin had become a badly-needed ally who could not be antagonised. He demanded that the 48% of Poland occupied by the Red Army in an act of aggression should become part of the Soviet Union. Poland's fate was sealed in Tehran in November 1943.

Meeting in secret, Churchill and Roosevelt gave in to Stalin's demands without the knowledge or participation of the exiled Polish Government. As a result, it was decided to assign Poland to the zone of influence of the Soviet Union after the war. It would lose its independence and territorial integrity.

The eastern part of Poland, the Kresy, from which the exiles who passed though Iran had been originally expelled and deported to labour camps, would be incorporated wholesale into the Soviet Union. The Poles were not even informed about this decision, lest it broke their fighting spirit. Ignorant of their fate, the free Polish Army continued to fight with the Allies, and over 48,000 lost their lives on Western battlefields.

The Tehran decision was officially confirmed at Yalta in February 1945, meaning that these soldiers had become homeless. After the war, they were scattered all over the world; over 110,000 settled in Britain and more in Australia, Canada and the USA.

The circumstances of their odyssey and the tragic history of the Polish people under Soviet occupation were hushed up by the Allies during this time to protect the reputation of the Soviet Union, an important ally in the war against the Nazis.

Roosevelt ordered General Earle to investigate Katyn in 1944. When he discovered the Soviet culpability Roosevelt ordered him to desist and reassigned him to Samoa.

During 1945-1990, Poland was gagged under Soviet control. A whole generation grew up not knowing of the plight of their country during the war.

Poland's Devastating Losses

In the immediate aftermath of World War Two, Poland was abandoned.

Between 1939 and 1945, over half a million fighting men and women and six million civilians lost their lives – approximately a fifth of the pre-war population.

Approximately 90% of Polish war losses were victims of prisons, death camps, raids, executions, starvation, excessive work and ill treatment.

Besides its human toll, the war left much of the country in ruins and inflicted indelible material and psychic scars. Poland lost 38% of its national assets, in comparison to Britain's 0.8% and France's 1.5%. Worse still, a part of Poland was also lost. The eastern provinces, annexed by the Soviets, included the two great Polish cities of Lwow and Wilno.

Among all the warring nations, statistics show that Poland

suffered the most devastation.

Polish citizens of various faiths, Catholic, Orthodox, Jewish, and Muslim, were arrested and deported from Eastern Poland in 1940-41 to special labour camps in Siberia, Kazakhstan and Soviet Asia. Less than one-third of the total number of deportees was thought to have survived.

As a result of the war, Pahlavi in Iran has one of the largest civil cemeteries in wartime. All the graves bear Polish names and the date "1942".

Many surviving deportees found their way out through Persia in 1942 as soldiers fighting in the free Polish Army under General Anders; many of their families eventually made their way west.

Following the amnesty, Polish soldiers in the west were deterred from returning to Poland, as they were branded traitors by the new Communist regime. Some soldiers who found their way back to Poland were arrested and imprisoned.

The final injustice was that, having the fourth largest combatant force fighting the Germans, Poland should have had a prominent place in the Victory parade in London. The Poles, however, and their crucial efforts, hardships and victories, were forsaken once again. The Polish soldiers were forced to watch from the sidelines as others marched triumphantly, even though they had taken a leading role in the defeat of Germany.

The irony?

Britain declared war on Germany because they invaded Poland.

19. GALLERY

Andrzej Gwizdak, 1920

Frank, Stasha, Andrzej in Puzieniewicze, 1922

Stasha (top left) and Gina (second row, middle)

Polish refugees crossing the Caspian Sea, 1942

Jozef in Scotland, 1943

Cheshek, 1948

Benek and Janina in Iran, 1943

Pola and Gina in Masindi, 1948

The Downarowicz brothers

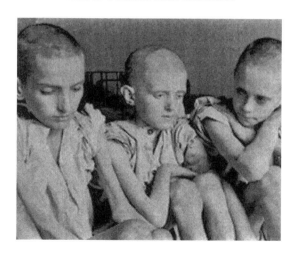

Polish orphans in Iran, 1942.

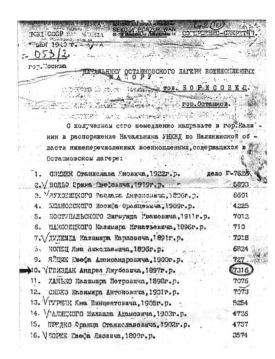

Stalin's death list featuring Andrzej Gwizdak's name

NKWD USSR
May 1940
058/2
Moscow

To Commandant of Ostashkow POW Camp
Major Comrade Borisowiec, Ostashkow

10.GWIZDAK Andrzej son of Jakub, born 1897, Case no 7316

СОВ. СЕКРЕТНО

СССР

**НАРОДНЫЙ КОМИССАРИАТ
ВНУТРЕННИХ ДЕЛ**

"___" марта 1940 г.
№ 794/Б

г. МОСКВА

Ц К   В К П (б)

товарищу С Т А Л И Н У

В лагерях для военнопленных НКВД СССР и в тюрьмах западных областей Украины и Белоруссии в настоящее время содержится большое количество бывших офицеров польской армии, бывших работников польской полиции и разведывательных органов, членов польских националистических к-р партий, участников вскрытых к-р повстанческих организаций, перебежчиков и др. Все они являются заклятыми врагами советской власти, преисполненными ненависти к советскому строю.

Военнопленные офицеры и полицейские, находясь в лагерях, пытаются продолжать к-р работу, ведут антисоветскую агитацию. Каждый из них только и ждет освобождения, чтобы иметь возможность активно включиться в борьбу против советской власти.

Органами НКВД в западных областях Украины и Белоруссии вскрыт ряд к-р повстанческих организаций. Во всех этих к-р организациях активную руководящую роль играли бывшие офицеры бывшей польской армии, бывшие полицейские и жандармы.

Среди задержанных перебежчиков и нарушителей гос-

т. Калинин - за
Каганович - за

Death warrant, signed by Stalin

213

Map of the Osadas in Baranowicze Province

Grave effects found at the excavation of Miednoye, 1991 to 1994

Lighters

Metal and pottery mugs

Grave effects found at the excavation of Miednoye, 1991 to 1994

Pipes and carved wooden boxes

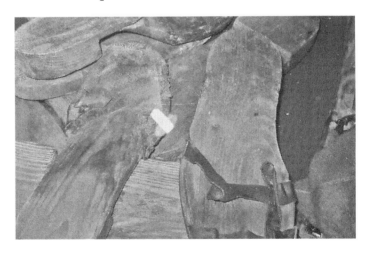

Wooden shoe soles

Guslawski	Franciszek	kapr.	Wolynskie	Luck	Rohyszcze	Dyminowka		Malachowce-Maczki Wolynskie
Gusstawski	Adam	por.	Bialostockie	Wolkowysk	Rus	Nowogrodki		
Guslowski	Ignacy	szer.	Wolynskie	Luck	Prazynia	Radomysl	7	
Guszczewicz	Kazimierz	ul.	Nowogrodzkie	Niedwiez	Zasalonowicze	Lochalnowicze	14	
Gutmarz	Dyonizy	ul.	Nowogrodzkie	Niedwiez		Zapalnia	3	
Gurman	Wladyslaw	plut.	Wolynskie	Luck				
Gutowski	A.	sierz.szt.	Poleskie	Pruzania	Nalezce	Milijowce	6	Tyniec Hallerowka
Guzowski	Jozef	plut.	Wolynskie	Rowne	Rowne	Hallerowka	3	
Gutowski	Franciszek	plut.	Wolynskie	Kowel	Suwk Koszaty	Stare Koszaty	12	Pruski Bakanowskie
Guzyrczyk	Tomasz	kapr.	Nowogrodzkie	Baranowicze	Ostrow	Bakanow		Pruski Bakanowskie
Gulyanzyk	Antoni	sbnz.	Nowogrodzkie	Baranowicze	Ostrow	Bakanow	13	Pruski Bakanowskie
Gulyanzyk	Andrzej	szer.	Nowogrodzkie	Baranowicze	Ostrow	Bakanow		
Guz	Edward	sierz.	Nowogrodzkie	Lida		Dunniatkowa		
Guz	Edmund	kapr.	Bialostockie	Wolkowysk		Harbow		Rutka
Guzek	Pawel	szer.	Wolynskie	Rowne	Tuczays	Pierzatkowka	41	Pitsuszczyzna
Guzewicz	Konstanty	kapr.	Wolynskie	Kostopol	Kostopol	Plaszowo	11	
Guzik	Stanislaw	plut.	Wolynskie	Dubno	Tenkadhow	Marysin	30	
Guzilkowski	Tadeusz	sierz.szt	Nowogrodzkie	Nowogrodzkie	Dworzec	Swintauzry	15	Luzingasatowka. Sulikowzazzyzna. Granatow
Guzowski	Alfons	kapr.	Wolynskie	Horochow	Charnow	Puzieniewicze	25	
Gwozdzik	Stanislaw	szer.	Nowogrodzkie	Grodno	Turzec			
Gwozdzik	Wladslaw	wachm.	Wolynskie	Rowne	Tuczyn	Pieningrad		
Gwozdzinski	Kazimierz	wachm.	Bialostockie	Slonim		Zasin	18	Jadlowiecka. Zaleskie
Gwozdz			Wolynskie	Rowne	Tuczys	Hallerowo		Zalen Nowy
Gwozdz	Jozef	sierz.	Wolynskie	Luck				Strzalkow
Halaj	Klemens	bomb.	Wolynskie	Krzemieniec	Dadperkdy	Duzo Zalnage	1	Siemkiewicze
Halberzak	Jozef	wachm.	Wolynskie	Luck	Polonka	Radomysl	5	Malachowce-Maczki Wolynskie
Halorin	Boleslaw	sierz.	Nowogrodzkie	Niedwiez		Ostra Gorka	8	
Halora	Jan	kapr.	Nowogrodzkie	Wolozyn				
Haczki	Zdzislaw	por.	Nowogrodzkie	Baranowicze	Stukowicze	Szlobowicze		
Haczynski	Wladyslaw	rtm.	Wolynskie	Wlodzimierz Wol.	Chadlaczhow	Fundum	10	
Hadala	Piotr	ogn.	Wolynskie	Horochow	Bereleterzdo	Namezyn	7	
Hader	Wladyslaw	plut.	Nowogrodzkie	Wolozyn				
Hagiel	Wladyslaw	chor.	Nowogrodzkie	Lida	Dokuatowo	Dzialkowice		
Hajbura	Andrzej	st.szer	Wolynskie	Horochow	Swiniuchy	Buzichow	28	Pomorzanska
Hajduk	Franciszek	szer.	Wolynskie	Krzemieniec	Bialozorka	Modelkow	33	Okle Gniazdto
Hajdak	Jan	plut.	Wolynskie	Luck	Podipejace	Wionatnislow		
Hajdukiewicz	Edward	gen.bryg.	Wolynskie	Dubno	Dubno	Krzywuzha	1	Romankow. Behrwalen. Armatkow
Hajdukiewicz	Stanislaw	st.szer	Nowogrodzkie	Lida	Lipnilazki	Mikolajko	6	
Hajdzich	Alfred	plut.	Wolynskie	Krzemieniec	Borsuki	Napadowka	12	
Hajdziony	Michal	szer.	Poleskie	Braniel. n/B	Wolozyn	Slawy	3	
Hajkiewicz	Jan	szer.	Wilenskie	Postawy	Kolewo	Karolinowo	8	
Hajsowicz	Dominik		Wilenskie	Oszmiana		Kamienica		

Land allocation detailing 25 hectares in Puzieniewicze awarded to Andrzej Gwizdak

Stasha's lament, a poem

You take my home
You take my living
Subject me to more
  take than giving

Deny my rights
Our basic needs
Destroy my hopes
'til my soul bleeds

I have my faith
I will not break
I have my God
He won't forsake

I see my child
Want is his eyes
Rags bind his feet
Death's lullabies

My son is gone
I will not heal
But must go on
  too numb to feel

I die inside
Another year
Where only lice
are thriving here

I won't despise
I'll be forgiving
Some hearts are dead
  but we are living

We take the roads
To who knows where?
We ride the rails
All things we share

I do my best
When there is none
Another day
  to see the sun

A thousand miles
A thousand more
A sadder world
  not as before

No state for us
This strangers' land
But where is home?
This place is sand

I have my dreams
I am not done
My own will thrive
  when I am gone

My life is ebbing
I slip away
This grave of water
My remains will stay.

A Memorial Plaque for Stanislawa Gwizdak, nee Downarowicz

As previously stated, Pahlavi in Iran has one of the largest civilian wartime cemeteries. The graves all bear Polish names and are dated 1942.

However, many like Stasha, who perished crossing the Caspian Sea, have nothing to mark their resting place.

In 2015, plans commenced to arrange for a further memorial in Pahlavi to commemorate the many whose bodies were committed to the Caspian Sea.

Jozef Jan Gwizdak's Ashes

My father's ashes are interred in the Polish communal grave in Stoney Road Cemetery in Halifax, West Yorkshire, as per his wishes.

However, we reserved a small amount and, two years after his death, took these ashes back to Poland and dispersed them into the River Vistula in Warsaw.

Part of his remains could then travel through the land of his birth and that of his forefathers.

Jozef and Doreen Gwizdak at a Polish dance held in West Vale, West Yorkshire, 1948

ABOUT THE AUTHOR

Marilyn Gwizdak Greenwood was born and brought up in the small town of Elland, West Yorkshire. She ran a number of successful businesses for many years, including a continental delicatessen, before moving into the healthcare sector. In retirement, she became a local councillor and now devotes her time to community issues and representing her constituents.

Printed in Great Britain
by Amazon